JANUA LINGUARUM

STUDIA MEMORIAE
NICOLAI VAN WIJK DEDICATA

edenda curat
C. H. VAN SCHOONEVELD
Indiana University

Series Practica, 175

A GRAMMAR OF SUBORDINATE STRUCTURES IN ENGLISH

by

ELDON G. LYTLE

1974

MOUTON

THE HAGUE · PARIS

LIBRARY OF CONGRESS CATALOG CARD NUMBER: 72-94485

Printed in Hungary

AUTHOR'S NOTE

In 1969 I received a grant from the Research Division of Brigham Young University to conduct research in syntax. The results of that research were reported in a monograph entitled *A Grammar of Subordinate Structures in English*. As it turned out, the monograph was sufficiently provocative to arouse the interest or ire of nearly all who read it. At the suggestion of Dr. Robert Blair, I offered the monograph to Mouton & Co. for publication. It was accepted, but a year passed before work on it could begin.

In the interim, the embryonic theory of language first presented in the monograph evolved rapidly, resulting eventually in a full-blown theory which is now being applied to problems in descriptive, contrastive, and computational linguistics. I have therefore revised the original report, to the extent that it could be done without starting from scratch, deleting some obnoxious passages, clarifying some points, and citing other documents now available which deal with various aspects of junction theory.

A sequel to the monograph is currently in preparation,[1] which will offer a more detailed exposition of the theory and its application. It will also contain a formalization of sufficient rigor, it is hoped, to make junction theory a more effective tool for dealing with the technical challenges which confront the modern linguist. I suspect that ultimately the comparative value of grammars will be assessed neither by some elegant evaluation metric, nor by how brilliantly we defend them, but by their utility in meeting the information and communication needs of a world society.

Many persons have contributed to the preparation of this study. In particular, I am grateful to Robert Blair, Rey Baird, Soren Cox, Alan Melby, and Sharon Jones for reviewing the manuscript. Thanks are also due to Ulla-Britta Melby for many long hours of typing. I alone, of course, am responsible for the content of these pages.

Eldon G. Lytle
Provo, Utah
December 1971

[1] Lytle and Melby, forthcoming.

FOREWORD

One cannot help but be impressed by the scope and variety of natural sentence structures. Whereas some might have once thought that a language is learned by memorizing its sentences, it is now clear that this is not possible. All normal humans possess the ability to form entirely new sentences, sentences no one has ever heard, read, or uttered before. This, of course, is the creative aspect of language to which adherents of the generative-transformational school of linguistics have repeatedly called our attention.[1]

The goal of this study is to describe certain subordinate structures in English and the generative mechanism, i.e. the grammar,[2] underlying their existence. Actually, the former should follow from the latter, but since the exact nature of this generative device is not obvious, linguists have attempted to discover its properties by analyzing the structures produced by it. Unfortunately, the linguist can seldom be certain that his analysis is entirely correct. It is a common experience to find that a hypothesis which accounts nicely for a significant class of structures fails to account for others which are clearly related. Moreover, the linguist can never be certain that he has not overlooked data which would cause him to revise or reject his analysis.

Difficulties of this sort have led linguists to be somewhat modest in their expectations. Rather than search for some universal discovery procedure whereby THE grammar of English (or any other human language) might be directly arrived at, it has been tacitly assumed that linguistic description of the same data may be non-unique. In other words, linguists often arrive at different and distinct sets of rules to account for the same data. Hence, some means is needed to determine which set of rules is to be most highly valued. This is the evaluation measure (or metric)

---

[1] The 'creative aspect' of language is discussed in every major work adhering to the generative-transformational point of view. See, for example, Chomsky, 1965, 1966.
[2] As in other recent literature, we use the word 'grammar' with systematic ambiguity. On the one hand, it denotes the speaker's internally represented linguistic competence. On the other hand, the linguist's description of that intrinsic knowledge is also referred to as a 'grammar'. For a discussion of COMPETENCE versus PERFORMANCE, see Chomsky, 1965.

frequently referred to in the literature.[3] The metric is intended to enable one to select
the 'best' grammar from among two or more grammars provided by the same theory
which appear to account equally well for the data.[4]

But here again, the linguist faces a dilemma. How is the optimum metric to be
obtained? There is no effective procedure for arriving at THE evaluation metric any
more than there is a discovery procedure for arriving at the optimum grammar.
Intuition suggests that economy and simplicity are the criteria to be applied. Unfortunately neither of these notions is an absolute provided outside of linguistic theory.[5]
The metric selected will determine the content of these notions, the selection of the
metric being an empirical matter. Hopefully, the optimum metric would correspond
in its evaluation to one's intuitive judgment, so that the rule labelled 'most general
(and, therefore, most simple)' by the metric will also be intuitively the most desirable.
At any rate, it is safe to assume that the grammar favored by the metric will not be
composed of independent and unrelated rules (i.e. *ad hoc* rules), each accounting for
a restricted set of structures, but that it will consist of 'teams' of rules which share
certain formal properties, each defined in relation to the others so that the whole
forms an integrated and rational system.

The linguist, therefore, does not approach the construction of grammars in a
haphazard fashion. In order to arrive at the synthesized and coherent system of rules
referred to above, he must have an explicit theory of linguistic structure upon which
to base the formalization of grammars.[6] The theory will suggest an analytical approach
to the data as well as formal properties of the rules and the overall format and integra-
tion of rule components. Ideally, the theory will not be language dependent, i.e.
restricted in its application to any particular language, but will define a class of
grammars adequate to describe human language in general.

This raises the question of HOW natural languages are similar and how they differ.
Grammarians have long been aware of the fact that in certain respects all natural
languages are similar. There has been renewed effort in recent years to isolate and
formalize linguistic universals. In fact, some current formalizations set up two
grammars – one containing language independent rules of universal validity, and.

[3] See Chomsky, 1965, or Chomsky and Halle, 1968, for a more detailed account of the evaluation
metric.
[4] Several grammars may be OBSERVATIONALLY adequate, i.e. they may appear to account equally
well for a finite set of primary data. A grammar which accounts not only for the data, but also for the
speaker's intrinsic linguistic competence is said to be DESCRIPTIVELY adequate. A linguistic theory
which provides a natural basis for the selection of descriptively adequate grammars is said to be
EXPLANATORILY adequate.
[5] Chomsky, 1965, 37–47.
[6] Most traditional grammatical descriptions are not sufficiently rigorous to meet the level of
descriptive adequacy because they lack an explicit theoretical basis. Pedagogical grammars often use
the organizational format elaborated for the description of Latin or other classical languages. Such
grammars concentrate on inflectional and conjugational paradigms with accompanying lists of
exceptions or irregularities. These, of course, are legitimate objects for grammatical description, but
the account given is generally superficial, relying to a considerable extent upon the student's intrinsic
intuition about linguistic structures to fill in the gaps.

another containing rules restricted in their validity to a particular language.[7] In syntax, one is led to suspect that the rules of the base component, i.e. those that generate basic sentence structures, are probably universal, whereas rules which determine superficial ordering and morphological (word) structuring are dependent upon particular languages.

It is the intent of this study to propose certain modifications of current syntactic theory and to investigate their consequences as they relate to linguistic universals. We make certain proposals about the generative mechanism which introduces subordinate constituents. These proposals are then applied to English in order to observe their effect and, eventually, to assess their validity.

[7] See Chomsky and Halle, 1968, for such an approach to the description of English Phonology.

TABLE OF CONTENTS

LIST OF SYMBOLS

Symbol	Meaning
A	Adjective or adverb
AdjP	Adjective phrase
AdvP	Adverb phrase
D	Label variable for the node of a subordinate structure which immediately dominates the intersect
E	The sememe in a lexical matching rule
Ø	Null sign
M	Node label for the comparative notions MORE and LESS
N	Noun
NP	Noun phrase
P	Preposition
PA	Predicate with an adjective or adverb nucleus
PdP	Predicate phrase
PP	Predicate with a preposition nucleus
PV	Predicate with a verb nucleus
Q	Quantifier
QP	Quantifier phrase
S	Sentence
SA	Predication with an adjective or adverb nucleus
SP	Predication with a preposition nucleus
SV	Predication with a verb nucleus
V	Verb
VP	Verb phrase
X	Node label variable
Y	Node label variable
Z	Node label variable

1

THEORETICAL ORIENTATION

LEVELS OF REPRESENTATION

Language must not be studied in a vacuum. To do so may lead to misconceptions about the structure of language and the nature of meaning. There is, for example, no such thing as an 'animate' noun or a 'transitive' verb.[1] Rather, there are nouns which denote objects which are presupposed to be animate and verbs which refer to transitive events. This fact has led certain linguists to define the meaning of a sentence as the total context in which it is uttered.[2] Words are symbols which derive meaning from the objects or relationships to which they refer.

The matter is more complex than this, however. There are multiple levels, or strata, of symbolic representation involved. Communication at the most primitive level involves the use of referents wherein the object or event itself is manipulated in such a way that the intended meaning is conveyed. In this case a physical context is actually created by the communicator.

The next level of symbolic representation apparently consists of mental images or concepts. Our sensory apparatus acquires and stores information about objects, events, and relationships perceived around us; thus the referential world is recorded and preserved at the conceptual level on the basis of perceptual experience.

The next level of symbolic representation seemingly consists of word images. As previously noted, words are symbols which depend upon their referents for meaning

---

[1] There are, of course, feminine or masculine nouns in many languages, but not female or male nouns. It is necessary in dealing with distinctive features to draw a distinction between features which are purely lexical (such as grammatical gender), and syntacto-semantic features which have referential substance.

[2] Bloomfield, 1933, 139. Chomsky apparently has this definition of meaning in mind when he states that to ask how syntax may be studied without reference to the meaning is tantamount to asking how syntax may be studied without reference to the hair-color of speakers (See Chomsky, 1957, 93). We abandon the strict dichotomy between syntax and semantics, believing them to be inextricably interwoven, and hence apply the compound SYNTACTO-SEMANTIC to the base component, as well as to distinctive features. It is not inconceivable that the hair-color of speakers might be highlighted in the idiom of some society where prestige, say, is determined by hair-color. We shall suggest how features of unlimited variety may be introduced into syntacto-semantic representations (See p. 44).

I. 'Real-world' objects, intrinsic or extrinsic, as perceived or presupposed by the speaker.

II. Mental objects corresponding to referents in Level I. This level of representation is language independent, its form and fabric a product of human perception.

III. Lexical objects corresponding to referents in Level II. Lexical signs are language specific.

IV. The oral or graphic level. The spoken or written word..

```
OBJECT ----------- SIGN (CONCEPT)
(SIGN)ᵃ              OBJECT ----------- SIGN (WORD IMAGE)
                                        OBJECT ----------- SIGN
```

Fig. 1.1. Each level of presentation serves as a basis for the next and so on successively until the level of articulated speech is achieved. The notion of language, meta-language, meta-meta-language . . . is familiar, of course, being characteristic of symbolic systems in general.

ᵃ In demonstration, objects represent themselves.

(in this case the mental representations just described, which are in turn based upon our perception of the world). When uttered or written, the word becomes an audible or visible sign, thus constituting the most superficial level of symbolic representation. Figure 1.1, p. 16, illustrates the various levels discussed.

Most grammarians before Humboldt apparently assumed that syntax was extra-linguistic in that to them it was merely a reflection of the structure of thought. Eventually, Humboldt and later Whorf, challenged this idea, suggesting that language itself is the vehicle of thought.[3] Linguistic relativity, the theory elaborated by these men, claims that a given language imposes a specific order of thought upon its speakers, so that our perception and thinking are determined by the form of the language we speak. To put it differently, these men believed that perception and thought are language dependent. Chomsky has used this same line of reasoning in recent years to place syntax securely within the realm of linguistic inquiry.[4]

The Whorfian hypothesis has been, and continues to be, controversial. We shall adopt the position that while limited language-specific influence may be active in our thinking, it is of minor significance when compared to inter-lingual similarities. In general we hold to the assumption that there does exist an independent level of thought upon which all languages are based (corresponding to Level II in Figure 1.1). Moreover, we assume that syntacto-semantic universals find their source at this level of representation, while linguistic differences originate at Level III, which we take to be the level where language-specific morphology is imposed.

The effect of this decision is not to exclude syntax from the realm of linguistic investigation. Whether syntax is linguistic or extra-linguistic is perhaps a pseudo-issue, since it reduces to the question of how LINGUISTICS is to be defined. A broad definition of the term as 'that discipline which studies the manipulation of signs for communication' is sufficient to bring all four levels within the range of the linguist.[5] Thus we might refer to demonstrative, mental, inner, and oral language as they correspond to Levels I–IV respectively.

What we have just suggested is not entirely novel. Other linguists of late have moved to abandon the level of representation used to represent deep structures within the framework of transformational grammar.[6] Accordingly, allusions are made to

---

[3] Waterman, 1964, and Carroll, 1964, discuss and evaluate the theoretical positions of these men. See also Chomsky, 1966 on Humboldt.

[4] Chomsky, 1965, 6–8.

[5] See Carroll, 1964, vii. Preface.

[6] Bach, 1968: "The hypothesis which I would like to entertain is that the base component does not actually add a phonological representation to the complex symbols of deep structure but merely develops the sets of semantic and syntactic features, which are then mapped into phonological shapes AFTER the operation of the transformational rules (or some part of the transformational rules) [117]. ... It should not be surprising that a system of universal base rules should turn out to be very close to such logical systems, which are after all the result of analyzing the most basic conceptual relationships that exist in natural languages. Such a system expresses directly the idea that it is possible to convey any conceptual context in any language, even though the particular lexical items available will vary widely from one language to another – a direct denial of the Humboldt-Sapir-Whorf hypothesis in its strongest form." (121–122).

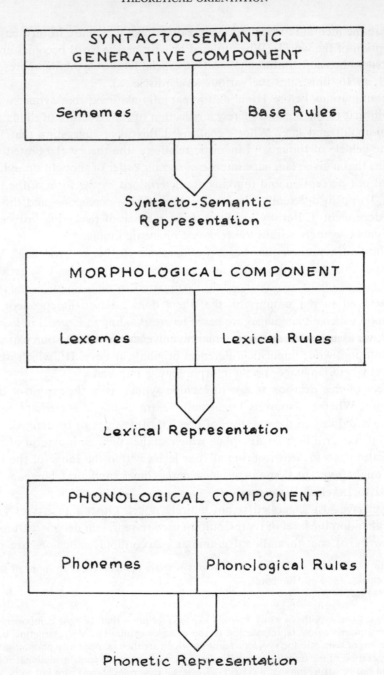

Fig. 1.2. The base rules operate with sememes (mental objects) to generate syntacto-semantic structures. Lexical rules operate with lexemes (lexical objects) to yield a phonological realization of Level II. Phonological rules operate with matrices of acoustical features (phonemes) to yield the phonetic representation of utterances.

generative semantics,[7] corresponding roughly to Level II, where the meaning of sentences, under the revised formulation is assumed to originate. This shift in thinking has been accompanied by increasing appeal to the notational conventions and formalism of symbolic logic.

The theoretical framework of this study corresponds to that of the modified hypothesis of deep structures last described.[8] Underlying representations correspond to Level II unless otherwise indicated. In order not to burden the reader with an excessive degree of abstraction, English words will be used in lieu of neutral semantic indices. Only those details immediately relevant to the discussion are annotated.[9]

We utilize familiar grammatical notation and terminology as much as possible. Constituent structure is given in the form of branching diagrams with labelled bracketing. As the discussion proceeds, certain relationships between independent and dependent structures will be redefined and notational modifications introduced where warranted. An alternate method for representing the structural relationship between antecedents and their modifiers is then introduced.

THE MODEL

A schema of the grammatical model we have sketched is given in Figure 1.2. The absence of a transformational component in the base is especially conspicuous, an abrupt departure from current generative theory, but certainly not an innovation within theoretical linguistics. For some time suggestions have been made to the effect that sentence structures ought to be obtainable directly, without recourse to transformations.[10] Transformationalists have responded with the challenge to construct such a grammar so that it can be examined and evaluated.[11] Attempts to do just that have been made, but so far are not enthusiastically received.[12]

The trend toward the elimination of transformations is unmistakable, however. Noam Chomsky, the author of generative-transformational theory, made a substantial

[7]   See Binnick, 1969, and the references given there.
[8]   Actually, this is a return to the pre-Humboldtian notion of deep structure with the exception that we now consider the structure of thought to be a legitimate object for linguistic description.
[9]   See Bach, 1968, and McCawley, 1968, for more detailed notation.
[10]   The term 'transformational rule' has been used broadly to refer to any grammatical rule which maps one level of linguistic representation into another within the context of a structural index. In this sense it is possible to formalize lexical insertion rules as substitution transformations (See Chomsky, 1965, 122–123). Clearly, it is not our intent to eliminate all grammatical rules falling within this broad definition. The particular transforms to be eliminated are those which alter structural relationships; others will be subsumed under different rubrics. In general, if we assign Level II rules the generative function and Level III rules the interpretive mapping-function, the scope of the transformational component is considerably reduced. Moreover, if a structure-preserving constraint is imposed upon transforms, residual transformational operations are eliminated. Thus, transformational rules are in effect absorbed by other rule components or disqualified.
[11]   Lees, 1966, xxxiv. Preface to the Third Printing.
[12]   See Šaumjan, 1964, and Rezvin, 1964. For a review of Šaumjan and Sobol'ova see Hall, 1963.

move in this direction himself with the elimination of generalized transformations. This was accomplished by incorporating an S-recursive rule (conjunction) into the phrase-structure grammar.[13] The introduction of distinctive features into syntactic deep-structures had a similar effect on certain singular transformations. Still more recently, Chomsky's lexical hypothesis proposes an expanded system of P-rules (phrase structure rules) in conjunction with certain lexical operations to partially supplant transformations in dealing with derived forms.[14] It seems that the discovery of linguistic generalities which permit other rules of grammar to supplant transformational functions constitutes sufficient justification for the elimination of the transforms involved. This manner of thinking is manifest by McCawley also, inasmuch as he proposes the elimination of certain conjunction-reduction transformations by applying set-theoretical operations in the base.[15]

We do not deny that basic sentence structures can be interrelated in various ways, but we reject the notion that once such relationships are defined, the resulting structures can be recast transformationally without altering modificational relationships and as a consequence, meaning, to some extent (See pp. 82–83). It will become apparent that embedding transformations become superfluous when a recursive mechanism of sufficient generality is incorporated into the phrase-structure grammar. The range of structures affected by such a mechanism is quite extensive, as will be seen. No entirely novel theoretical or methodological approach is required to achieve these results. The precedent for subordinating constituents by means of phrase-structure rules is provided by the rule NP → NP S, which will undergo revision and generalization.

Other transformational functions will be supplanted by lexical operations. This has the effect of relegating language specific operations to Level III, where a language dependent lexicalization is imposed. Although no detailed account is given of the lexical rules which map language-independent semantic deep-structures into language-specific lexical strings, an illustrative set of lexical rules is given in Appendix I. Such rules are assumed to exist for each language and are claimed to be responsible for word order and morphological structuring. The relative number and complexity of these rules will be a function of specific languages, although universal constraints no doubt come into play. Syntacto-semantic features required for the environment of context-sensitive lexical rules are provided by Level II, as is the constituent structure necessary for the placement of derivational affixes and the subsequent application of phonological rules. It may be stated at this point that rules of the type suggested appear adequate to yield lexical realizations of morphologically complex languages such as Mam.[16]

---

[13]   Chomsky, 1965, 128–137.
[14]   Chomsky, 1969.
[15]   McCawley, 1968.
[16]   Robertson, 1969, 36–37.

2

JUNCTION

BASIC GRAMMATICAL OPERATIONS

The creative aspect of language previously noted stems largely from recursive processes of junction. We postulate at least three basic operations which apply at Level II to combine sememes into meaningful expressions. These are ADJUNCTION, CONJUNCTION, and SUBJUNCTION.

ADJUNCTION. We use this term to designate the relationship between subjects and predicates, and between predicators and objects[1] in the sentence. In *The cat scratched me*, *The cat* is adjoined to *scratched me; scratched* is in turn adjoined to *me*:[2]

The rules generating the above structure are familiar as rewrite rules: S→NP PdP; PdP→VP NP. We shall let the familiar expression X→YZ represent the adjunctive process.

---

[1] 'Subject', 'predicate', and 'object' are used here in their usual grammatical sense. 'Predicator' is employed to denote the nuclear element of predicates, i.e. verbs, adjectives, adverbs, and prepositions. For further discussion see Chapter 6.
[2] See list of symbols for meaning of node labels, p. 13.

CONJUNCTION. This operation entails joining constituents on the same structural level in such a way that they form a collection of objects conceived as a whole. In other words, constituents which are conjoined constitute the elements of a broader constituent. For example, the expression *the dog and the cat* is an NP consisting of two conjoined NP's.

Rule: NP→NP and NP

The compound sentence *John washed and Mary dried* is a sentence formed by compounding two sentences.

Rule: S→S and S

The compound expression *Write Spanish and speak Russian* is a predicate phrase consisting of two conjoined predicate phrases.

Rule: PdP→PdP and PdP

By using cover symbols (variables) for the category symbols in the rewrite rules

$$NP \rightarrow NP \text{ and } NP$$

$$PdP \rightarrow PdP \text{ and } PdP$$

$$S \rightarrow S \text{ and } S,$$

which generate conjoined structures, we can conflate them into a single formula:

$$X \rightarrow X \text{ and } X.$$

This is simply a claim that conjunction is a very general operation which combines elementary constituents into compounded ones. Since compounds may contain more than two sub-parts, the rule expressing the conjunctive process must be generalized further to allow an unlimited number of conjoined constituents:

$$X \rightarrow X \text{ (and } X)_1^n$$

The notation is intended to mean that at least one constituent (sub-script) must be conjoined to another if conjunction occurs, while no upper limit is imposed at all (super-script).

Note that the structure-preserving constraint we have placed on grammatical rules excludes the generation of compounds via the conjunction-reduction process familiar in transformational grammar. This does not preclude lexical hiatus, however, which does not entail structural change (see Appendix I).

SUBJUNCTION. This form of junction is our central concern. It is our contention that subjunction is a distinct operation resulting in relationships which are different from those resulting from adjunction or conjunction. We assert that it is not possible to generate subordinate constituents by adjoining them to their antecedents. Furthermore, it is our conviction that the failure of modern theoreticians to acknowledge the authenticity of the traditional concept of subordination as distinct from other types of junction has hindered the progress of descriptive syntax and semantics.[3]

The following paragraphs are devoted to a reappraisal of the rule NP→NP S (the relative clause rule) and to a reinterpretation of its formal properties. Subjunction will then be generalized to account for a variety of subordinate constructions.

The SUBORDINATE RELATIONSHIP. Transformationalists have assumed that the operation symbolized by the rule NP→NP S merely adjoined a relative clause (the S) to an antecedent NP, both of these being subtended by the NP appearing to the left of the

---

[3] The three forms of junction proposed in this study can be explicated in terms of categorial patterning. For further discussion see Lytle and Melby, forthcoming.

arrow:

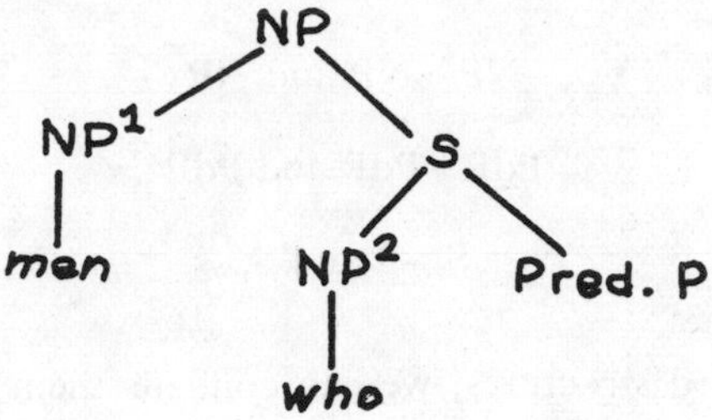

There is an identity condition imposed upon the antecedent (NP[1] of the example) and some constituent of the embedded sentence (NP[2] in this case) to account for the referential identity of the relative pronoun and its antecedent. Transformations replace NP[2] with a relative pronoun, or, in some instances, delete it entirely (*the boy* [*whom*] *we saw* . . .), and accomplish any necessary re-ordering of constituents.

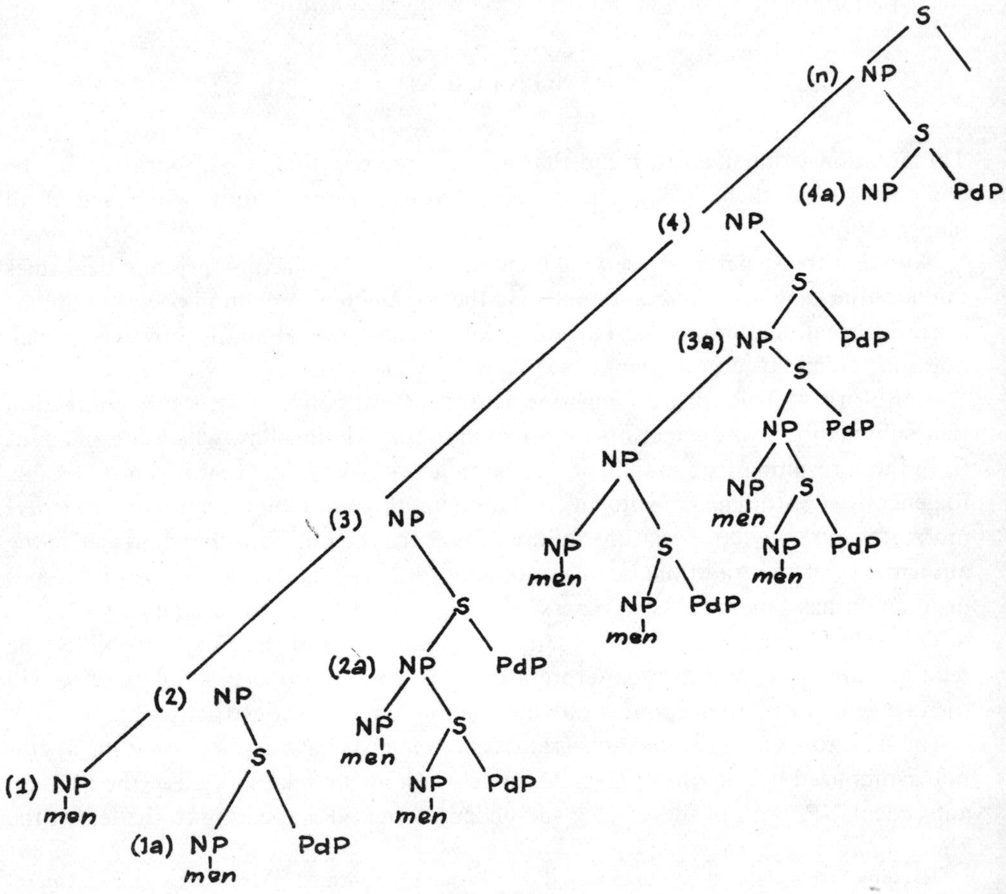

Fig. 2.1

This analysis seems straightforward until we attempt an explication of relative clause sequences:

> (1) Men who[1] are rich who[2] are generous who[3] ... who[n] ... are a blessing to society.

In order to satisfy the NP identity condition, the phrase marker shown in Figure 2.1 is constructed. Notice the multiple occurrences of NP.[4]

NP's (1) and (1a) are identical. Similarly, NP's (2) and (2a) are identical. Underlying *men, who[1] ... who[2] ... who[3]* are eight (8) occurrences of *men*. The odd number of nominal constituents in the surface structure is due to the fact that the antecedent of the second relative pronoun is NP (2), which contains two occurrences of *men* rather than a single occurrence; similarly, the antecedent of *who[3]* is NP (3), which contains four occurrences of *men*, and so on. After the first relative pronoun, there is not a one-to-one correspondence between pronouns and underlying occurrences of *men*, but the progressive relationship depicted in Figure 2.2.

The number of occurrences of *men* is simply doubled for each successive term in the relative sequence. The number of underlying occurrences of the 'head-noun' (*men* in this instance) can be calculated for a given relative pronoun by raising *2* to the power corresponding to its ordinal position *n* in the sequence (see the super-scripts on the

---

[4]   Yet another alternative which circumvents structural proliferation gives the following P-marker for sentence (1):

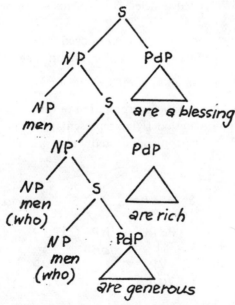

Still another alternative would be to require that the relativized sentence contain an NP coreferential with the antecedent NP, rather than identical to it. Although alternatives such as these are attractive, they do not circumvent the embedding of S into NP, a relation we wish to reserve for certain nominalizations.

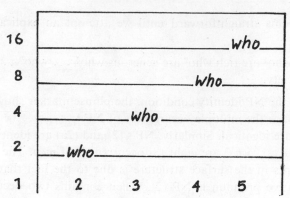

Fig. 2.2. The horizontal column represents the ordinal position of the relative pronoun in the sequence. The vertical column shows number of *men* occurrences underlying the antecedent of the relative pronoun.

pronouns in sentence [1]). We are considering, then, a progression of the order 2^n. If set indices are admitted in underlying syntacto-semantic representations, an ascending cardinality of this order is not unexpected. We might explain it as a manifestation of those sets, 2^n being the formula which expresses the number of elements in power sets (the family of all the subsets of any set X is called the POWER SET of X). The proliferation of structure involved does pose a serious problem for the lexicalization process, however. The multiplicity of underlying constituents must be monitored for identity and rules formulated to delete constituents which have no lexical realization.

Conjunction reduction transformations have been proposed to deal with a similar problem in conjoined structures. Consider, for example, the rather trivial sentence

(2) Dick and Jane run and jump.

In order to account for the semantic interpretation of this sentence, transformational grammarians have proposed an underlying representation consisting of four distinct sentences (see Figure 2.3). The conjunction reduction process monitors the identity

Fig. 2.3

of constituents and deletes some of them, reducing deep-structure representation until it assumes the surface form familiar to us.

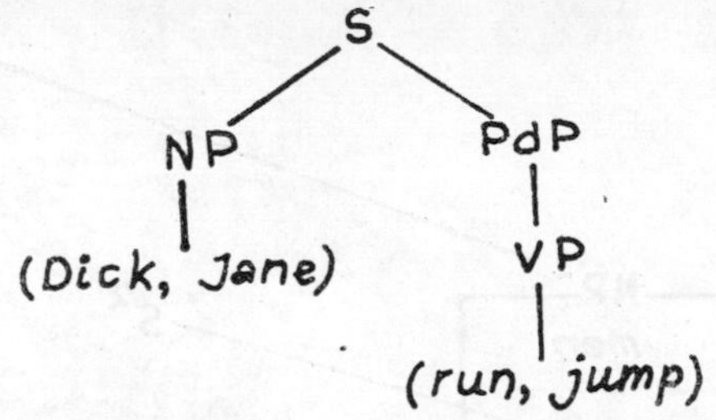

Fig. 2.4

The problem may be approached from another angle, however. Given the presence of set indices in semantic representations, the four sentences shown in Figure 2.3 (corresponding to sentence [2]) can be explained as a predictable manifestation, the Cartesian product, of set indices underlying surface constituents: Given the sets NP and PdP depicted above, a Cartesian product exists for them consisting of the following pairs: *(Dick, run)*, *(Dick, jump)*, *(Jane, run)*, *(Jane, jump)*. It is these pairs which motivate the four underlying sentences shown in Figure 2.3. There is, however, no *a priori* reason for selecting a product manifestation as the basis for lexical interpretation. It is far simpler to use NP and PdP as they appear in Figure 2.4. Their expansion into a product set may be considered to be a process of semantic interpretation quite independent of lexicalization. A similar solution suggests itself for dealing with relative clause sequences. If we can discover what the disposition of set indices underlying such sequences is like, we can use them as a basis for lexicalization and disregard their power-set manifestation.

A closer examination of the phrase marker given in Figure 2.1 permits one to observe that the specific constituent relationship which forces structural proliferation is the sequential embedding of entire S constituents into NP's. Since the identity condition (between antecedents and prospective pronominal constituents) is defined on NP's, each newly embedded S figures in the identification of subsequent NP's introduced into the sequence. It is our belief that the above is an incorrect interpretation of the structure underlying relative clauses. We propose that only an NP of the relative clause is embedded into the matrix NP, resulting in the structural relationships depicted in Figure 2.5. The revision proposed has several immediate consequences of significance: (1) There is no proliferation of nodes, and, consequently, (2) the suppression of superfluous constituents is not necessary. This means that (3) there is a one-to-one correspondence between underlying NP occurrences and their lexical manifestation (unless relative pronouns are omitted during the lexicalization process). (4) The task of determining constituent identity is simplified because (5) the node of the relative clause linked by subjunction to the main clause will always be coreferential with the antecedent to which it is joined. We shall return to this latter point directly.

We shall use this revised relative structure as a basis for differentiating between adjunction and subjunction. Note that no two NP's in Figure 2.5 are on the same structural level. We stipulate that NP^2 is not an adjunct of NP^1, but is SUBJOINED

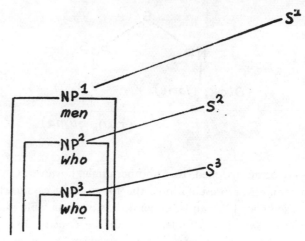

Fig. 2.5. The structure of a relative clause sequence.

to it. In order to maintain this distinction, we reinterpret the relative clause rule to read:

NP subjoin NP of S

and modify the notation of the rule to NP/NP S. The junction formed by the application of this rule is characterized by the simultaneous participation of the same referent at both super- and subordinate levels in such a way that it forms a POINT OF REFERENTIAL FOCUS, a link between structural levels. In subsequent illustration, we shall designate the subordinate relationship by a vertical line.[5] Adjuncts and conjuncts are annotated in the customary manner.

Having introduced subjunction as a distinct operation, we are obliged to demonstrate its generality. Accordingly, we generalize the relative clause rule by using variables:

X/X S

By replacing the variables with specific category symbols (NP, PdP, VP, AdjP, AdvP), we predict that subordinate clauses corresponding to the following specializations of the formula exist in English (and in human languages generally):

  a. NP/NP S (noun phrase relatives)
  b. PdP/PdP S (predicate phrase relatives)
  c. VP/VP S (verb phrase relatives)
  d. AdjP/AdjP S (adjective phrase relatives)
  e. AdvP/AdvP S (adverb phrase relatives)

Before demonstrating the existence of these various types of subordinate clauses, we shall digress to discuss other relevant matters. First we shall offer additional motiva-

---

[5] There is considerable evidence to indicate that the 'geometric' distinction between junction forms utilized in this study can and should be supplanted by distinctions based on categorial predominance (see Lytle, 1971; and references given in Footnote 3 above). The representation utilized herein is sufficient for our present purpose, however.

tion for the revised interpretation of relative structures we have proposed. Secondly, we shall consider the restrictive-nonrestrictive dichotomy characteristic of grammatical modifiers and attempt to explain this phenomenon in a manner consistent with the theoretical framework elaborated thus far.

NONRESTRICTIVIZATION

It seems unlikely that an independent and distinct act of reference underlies every occurrence of *men* in Figure 2.1. Logically, a restrictive sequence of the type being considered would permit unique identification of a referent by relating it to a multiplicity of facts in a single act of reference. In other words, it seems natural to suppose that sequential subordination is a linguistic device for achieving REFERENTIAL FOCUS. Actually, there is empirical evidence that such is the case. Let us examine briefly a linguistic phenomenon which we shall term NONRESTRICTIVIZATION. By nonrestrictivization we mean that when allusion is made more than once to the same referent in a given context, the sememe-lexeme relationship becomes unique, so that subsequently only nonrestrictive relative clauses occur in conjunction with that constituent.[6] Nonrestrictivization is an observable result of referential focus. Violation of this principle forces an interpretation wherein the referent changes. Consider the following sentences:

(3a) The Smiths have a boy and a girl.

(3b) The boy, who is ten, delivers our paper.

(3b′) The boy who is ten delivers our paper.

(3c) We saw a doe and a buck, but the buck, which was a four-point, outsmarted us.

(3c′) We saw a doe and a buck, but the buck which was a four-point, outsmarted us.

The referent of *boy* in (3b) is understood to be the same person mentioned in (3a); the boy referred to in (3b′), however, has to be an entirely different person. Similarly, (3c′) is semantically anomalous if the second occurrence of *buck* is intended to have the same referent as the first. Sentences (3a) and (3b), as well as (3c) demonstrate both definitization and nonrestrictivization. The only apparent exceptions to the rule are (1) where there is verbatim repetition of the restrictive(s) first used to identify the referent; or (2) where intervening discourse creates a need for reacquiring referential focus:

(4a) The Smiths have a boy who is ten and a boy who is six.

(4b) The boy who is ten, who delivers our paper, is named Fred.

(4c) The boy who is ten who delivers our paper is named Fred.

(4d) The Smith boy whom I mentioned who is ten....

---

[6] See Kuroda, 1968, 254–255, regarding DEFINITIZATION, which is related if not identical to what we have termed NONRESTRICTIVIZATION.

Notice that (4c) presupposes a shift of referent. Interestingly, lexical identity does not seem to be a factor in nonrestrictivization at all. Referential identity is sufficient in the following sentences:

> (5a) I bought a new car, but that pile of junk, which is a luxury model, by the way, broke down the next day.
>
> (5b) A man and a boy were fishing, but the lad, who was only twelve, caught more fish than his uncle, who was thirty-two.

Returning now to sentence (1) and its underlying representation of relative sequences, note that multiple allusions to the same referent are implied, especially in the expanded representations. If each occurrence of a particular referent were regarded as a complete and distinct act of reference, it is difficult to see why nonrestrictivization would not occur promptly, i.e. upon the second occurrence of *men*. This suggests that a single act of reference is better regarded as a process of constructing a lexical representation which uniquely satisfies a syntacto-semantic representation than as a function of how many times a particular referent appears in underlying representation. However, a synthesis of both points of view is not out of the question either. A re-evaluation of the structural posture of referents occurring at the junction of super- and subordinate clauses is possible. Specifically, we could postulate that the link between structural levels is a single occurrence of a given referent such that it functions simultaneously in overlapping constituents. The revisions we have proposed provide a structure for which such an interpretation is plausible (See Figure 2.5). Lexical reinterpretation of the same element corresponding to its multiple functions would account for pronominal forms at the lexical level. As an illustration of how this latter point of view differs from the former, consider the following sentences:

> (6a) The steak you prefer is expensive.
>
> (6b) What disappoints me most is the bad weather.

From the latter point of view, the missing pronouns in these sentences (*that* and *that which* respectively) are explained on the basis that lexical reinterpretation did not occur, as opposed to the idea that separate and distinct constituents which might yield them have been deleted.

We shall consider nonrestrictivization as it relates to the status of modifiers in more detail at a later point in the discussion.

SYNTACTIC INTERSECTION

In conjunction with our interpretation of the structure underlying relative clauses, we introduce the concept of syntactic intersection. It is convenient to conceptualize super- and subordinate structures as intersecting at a particular constituent. The shared constituent forms the junction between structural levels and forms the point of referential focus. To date, only restrictive relative clauses have been recognized by TG as sharing an element with the main clause (the antecedent of the relative pronoun) in such a way that the subordinate structure is associated with an antecedent in the deep structure. It appears, however, that intersection is actually a very general phenomenon, as we shall attempt to demonstrate in subsequent chapters.

PHONOLOGICAL PHRASING

Other evidence in favor of the interpretation we have proposed for the structure of relative clauses is the apparent solution it offers for problems which have arisen with regard to phonological phrasing. It has been stated, for example, that

... in reading the right-branching construction "this is the cat that caught the rat that stole the cheese", the intonation breaks are ordinarily inserted in the wrong places (that is, after "cat" and "rat"...).[7]

The phrasing to be expected in terms of NP→NP S is: [*This is* [*the cat that caught* [*the rat that stole the cheese*]]]. Readjustment rules have been suggested to account for the fact that actual phrasing places intonation breaks after *cat* and *rat* rather than in the positions shown.[8] Note, however, that the constituent break yielded by the relations we have defined corresponds in each case to the intersect marking the junction between super- and subordinate sentences: *This is the cat: that caught the rat: that stole the cheese*. We suspect that the discrepancy between actual and predicted phrasing reduces to a misinterpretation of syntactic structure rather than to the operation of other intermediary rules.

HETEROGENEOUS SUBJUNCTION UNDERLIES DERIVATION

The structural modifications for relative sequences proposed above are crucial for yet another reason. The embedding of an entire constituent within a node of different grammatical category (i.e. a heterogeneous subjunction) would hopefully result in derivation, as, for example, the active nominalization in English *(John's death...)*, where a verb phrase is actually embedded in a nominal phrase. We shall attempt to show how the internal structure of complex derived forms can be provided naturally if the revisions we have made are pursued to their logical conclusion. We suggest that the inclusion of an entire S within an NP (as provided by the usual interpretation of the rule NP→NP S) would yield a nominalization of the clause. The modified structure of relatives we have given averts this unacceptable result.

Again we stipulate, however, that we must revise our interpretation of the relative clause rule. It can no longer be viewed as a rewrite rule which simply segments one constituent into adjoined subconstituents. Rather it must be considered to be a special syntactic operation which acts selectively to embed constituents within others

[7] Chomsky, 1965, 13.
[8] Chomsky and Halle, 1968, 371–372.

in such a way that subordinate structures are introduced and explicitly related to constituents in the superordinate structure.

Let us now turn to a more detailed consideration of the restrictive-nonrestrictive dichotomy found in relative modifiers. First we will review the transformational point of view with regard to nonrestrictives; then we shall elaborate our own position.

THE TRANSFORMATIONAL POINT OF VIEW

A great deal has been said and written about relative clauses. Every student hears sooner or later that a restrictive clause limits the scope of the noun, and cannot be extracted from the matrix sentence without altering its meaning. On the other hand, he learns that a nonrestrictive clause can be recognized by the pauses that set it off from the remainder of the structure, and that a nonrestrictive clause can be removed without altering the semantic interpretation of the matrix sentence. Generally speaking, transformationalists have attempted to explicate such observations within their own theoretical framework. Recent generative studies have claimed that restrictive clauses result from the rule NP→NP S. However, nonrestrictive clauses are derived transformationally from conjoined sentences. We quote Lakoff:

The difference in function between restrictive and non-restrictive clauses is well-known. As their names suggest, restrictive clauses limit the scope of the noun phrases they are associated with, while non-restrictive clauses do not. ... Restrictive clauses, since they limit noun phrases must be closely related to them in the deep structure. Peters and I have argued that they are introduced by a phrase structure rule of the form NP → NP S. Others have argued that they are introduced as a part of the determiner constituent inside of the NP. Non-restrictive clauses, on the other hand, serve no limiting function and so there is no reason to believe that they are associated with noun phrases in the deep structure ... there must be a rule that takes a sentence from a conjoined structure and adjoins it to a noun phrase. This is just the kind of rule that we would need if we were to form non-restrictive relative clauses from conjoined sentences. In fact, we would claim that appositive clauses are intermediate steps in the derivation of non-restrictive clauses. ...[9]

The derivation proposed by Lakoff would include the following intermediate steps:

      (a) Even John left early and he is a friend of mine.
      (b) Even John, and he is a friend of mine, left early.
      (c) Even John, who is a friend of mine, left early.

The underlying structure for all three sentences would be:

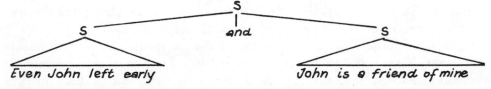

Jacobs and Rosenbaum defend the same point of view:

The difference between restrictive relative clauses ... and nonrestrictive clauses should be apparent from the sentences below:

---

[9]   Lakoff, 1966, 64–65. Quoted from a revised version of Lakoff, 1965. Ditto copy.

professors who enjoy poetry are idealistic
professors, who enjoy poetry, are idealistic.

These sentences differ in a number of ways. . . . The first sentence is a single assertion about a certain subclass of professors; only those who enjoy poetry. The assertion is that such professors are idealistic. But the second makes two assertions: that *all* professors are idealistic and that *all* professors like poetry. It is characteristic of nonrestrictive relative clauses that they are interpreted as assertions which could stand in their own right as independent sentences without changing the meaning of the sentences in which they appear. Thus, the assertion

professors are idealistic

has the same meaning in the compound sentence

professors are idealistic and professors enjoy poetry

as it does in the sentence

professors, who enjoy poetry, are idealistic.

On the other hand, if a restrictive clause is removed, the meaning of the sentence in which it appears will be completely changed.
Restrictive clauses are generated from a sentence embedded in a noun phrase containing another noun phrase. Nonrestrictive clauses are independent conjoined sentences introduced into noun phrases by the nonrestrictive clause transformation.[10]

In the following section we will test the validity of the transformational point of view in the context of other pertinent observations.

ENVELOPE FEATURES

Developments in transformational grammar have led to the elimination or restructuring of some transforms by introducing certain syntactic markers in the deep structure. Thus, a question marker (Q), introduced as an optional element by the base rules, obviates the need for the original question transformations. Likewise, an imperative marker obviates the need for a transform to introduce this element. This approach derives from the condition that transformations may not change meaning.[11] The introduction of Q by a transform would obviously violate this condition. Similarly such alternations as SING/PLUR, PAST/FUTURE, DEFINITE/INDEFINITE, must be dealt with in such a way that transforms need not introduce or delete them. Thus, syntactic features like these were incorporated into base rules, and are now used to govern alternations such as the above, relieving the transformational component of this particular function. Features such as Q, which may envelop entire sentences, we will refer to as ENVELOPE FEATURES.

Envelope features provide strong evidence for the independence of relative and conjoined structures. As previously pointed out, such features have semantic value and must be present in the deep structure for semantic interpretation before trans-

[10] Jacobs and Rosenbaum, 1968, 259–260.
[11] Katz and Postal, 1964, 74.

formations apply. The question to be resolved, then, is this: Where, precisely, must envelope features be attached? In order to illustrate the difficulties involved, let us consider this question as it relates to a specific nonrestrictive modifier:

(7a) Are professors, who enjoy poetry, idealistic?

We ask: What is the deep structure of this sentence? One's first inclination is to introduce Q at the highest S. This, however, would involve both constituent sentences in the interrogative, which would yield

(7b) Are professors idealistic and do they (professors) enjoy poetry?

This, then, is not the correct deep structure for the example sentence. Assuming that Q is defined at the secondary rather than the primary level, we could have either

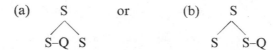

Structure (a) would yield:

(7c) *Are professors idealistic (?) and they enjoy poetry.

This is a more interesting possibility. It is still troublesome, however. Although the constituent sentences show the correct distribution of envelope features (the potential matrix is interrogative and the embedding prospect declarative), a grammatically well-formed conjunction of the two is not possible. It seems somewhat paradoxical that a grammatically well-formed transform (the nonrestrictive) cannot occur grammatically in its base form (conjunction). A parallel situation would be a grammatical passive structure for which no grammatical active correspondence can be cited. We might argue that certain conditions make the transform obligatory, but this strikes one as simply a way out without really solving the problem. Alternatively, we might consider the deep structure of the example sentence to be:

(7d) Professors enjoy poetry, but are they idealistic?

But the semantic equivalence of this sentence to the nonrestrictive is questionable.

Still another objection can be offered against (a): The deep structure shows the entire structure as non-interrogative (the highest S), whereas the example sentence is clearly enveloped by an interrogative. It might be argued that the potential matrix S becomes the highest S after the embedding and subsequent pruning, but this is unsatisfactory – semantic interpretation is based on deep structure, not derived structure. Alternative (b) attaches Q to the wrong clause but brings to our attention a significant fact: relative clauses are declarative. They are not normally interrogative or imperative (See p. 53 on interrogative shift). The conjoined version of (b) gives:

(7e) *Professors are idealistic and do they enjoy poetry?

In order to avert the awkwardness, 'but' would have to be used:

"Professors are idealistic, but do they enjoy poetry?"

This introduces a contrastive element which is not intended, however. The relative version is still more improbable:

(7f) *Professors, (do) who enjoy poetry (?), are idealistic.

An appositive, which Lakoff postulates as an intermediate step between the conjoined structure and the nonrestrictive is more tolerable,

(7g) Professors – do they enjoy poetry? – are idealistic.

but marginally so. Moreover, an analysis which proposes three steps, of which the initial and final steps are ungrammatical, seems less than satisfactory.

IMPLICATIONS OF THE PROBLEM

None of the deep structures proposed above as the origin of nonrestrictive relative clauses is entirely satisfactory, unless we relax the condition that transformations may not change meaning (the domain of Q in this case). A decision to this effect would return us to the original position of transformational grammar, namely, that not even the weakest semantic relation holds in general between kernel and transform.[12] This, of course, is diametrically opposed to the currently accepted condition, that transforms may not change meaning. It is doubtful that we would want to go that far. An intermediate position suggests itself, i.e. that transforms be permitted to change meaning, but not arbitrarily. But this is obscure at best. What types of meaning are there? Which meanings will transforms be permitted to alter, or, perhaps, define? Certainly transforms cannot be permitted to change the 'hair-color of speakers', i.e. meaning defined as the situation in which an utterance occurs. If we could begin in the deep structure with essentially neutral structures, and permit transforms to arrange them with relation to each other while simultaneously defining the distribution of envelope features, this would perhaps be neither drastic nor arbitrary: Structural meaning would be subject to definition by transforms, but referential meaning would remain intact. But then we would have to show that situation has no inherent structural posture.[13] The difficulty of clarifying the matter is all too obvious.

Alternatively, we would have to assume that all relatives and conjoined structures are independently generated in the deep structure and forsake the notion that one is derived from the other. This would circumvent the difficulty discussed above, where transformational re-structuring seems incompatible with the distribution of envelope features. This is the position we have adopted.

---

[12]   Chomsky, 1957, 101.
[13]   See discussion regarding the structure of reference, pp. 81–83.

At any rate, the two alternatives (See Figures 2.8 and 2.9) presented are at opposite extremes of the spectrum. On the one hand, we are unable to show how kernel structures can be rearranged transformationally without resulting in an anomalous distribution of envelope features. On the other hand, no one has shown how the vast

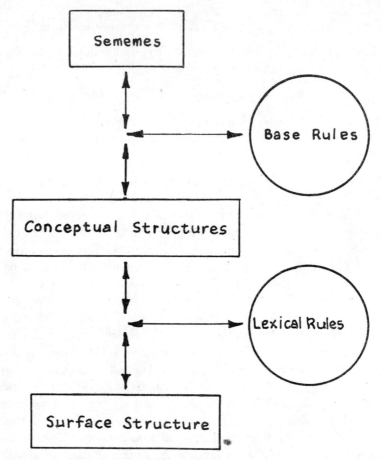

Fig. 2.8. The DIRECT generation of syntactic structure is accomplished by base rules which join sememes into meaningful units. Other rules of grammar INTERPRET that structure BUT MAY NOT ALTER IT.

variety of syntactic structures can be directly generated. At present, linguists seem to be compromising between the two approaches. But is such compromise really the answer?

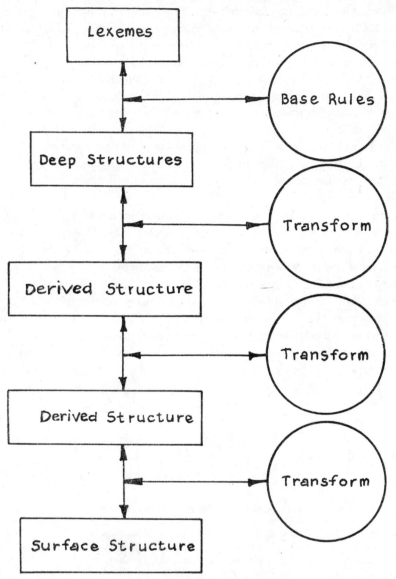

Fig. 2.9. The INDIRECT generation of structure is accomplished by transforming the output of base rules into a variety of derived phrase markers.

THE SEMANTIC ARGUMENT

The whole issue, of course, revolves around questions of meaning. A review of typical arguments used to defend transformational analyses leaves one with the impression that we have too often made claims about semantics without having any formal

method for making semantic measurements. For example, it is a common argument
that sentences having IDENTICAL semantic interpretations derive from the same deep
structure. Indeed, this is the nucleus for arguments quoted above alleging that nonrestrictive clauses derive from conjoined sentences.[14] How does one judge semantic
equivalence without a thorough explication of meaning? The reply to this crucial
question is simply that one must rely on linguistic intuition. But what if a sample
of our best linguistic intuition is not unanimous? Each linguist is entitled to his own
opinion, of course.

It should be evident that semantic arguments tend to be inconclusive. In order to
demonstrate the type of pitfalls one encounters, let us reconsider the same data
employed to motivate the conjoined-origin postulate for nonrestrictives, but in conjunction with certain other observations.

Briefly, the semantic argument is as follows: The sentence *professors, who enjoy
poetry, are idealistic* is semantically identical to *professors enjoy poetry and professors
are idealistic*. Each sentence makes the same allegations about the same referents.
Each can stand alone in its own right. This is evidenced by the fact that the embedded
nonrestrictive clause can be removed without changing the meaning of the matrix:
professors are idealistic. The same is not true of the corresponding restrictive *professors
who enjoy poetry are idealistic*. A conjoined paraphrase is not found for it, and removal
of the restrictive clause alters the semantic interpretation of the matrix (the scope of
professors changes from *some* to *all*). This suggests that the restrictive clause must
have been in place in the deep structure. Otherwise, the relative transform which
embedded it there would violate the meaning-change condition (*all → some*).

But suppose that we were to discover a conjoined structure with a semantic interpretation *equivalent* to that of the restrictive relative? By the same token, i.e. by
reason of semantic IDENTITY, we would have to conclude that restrictive clauses also
derive from conjoined sentences in the deep structure.

---

[14]   One should not get the impression that semantics is the sole basis for transformational arguments.
Transformationalists have always recognized the difficulty of explicating meaning and sought to
provide syntactic motivation for their analyses. In fact, it was Chomsky's initial intent to divorce the
construction of grammars from appeals to meaning (See Chomsky, 1957, 92–105). As research
proceeded, however, it became apparent that semantic interpretation would have to be handled by
generative grammar, and a semantic component was incorporated into the model. Early work suggested that semantics could be equated with a residue not accounted for by the syntactic component.
This approach proved untenable, however, since a conclusive formalization of the syntactic domain
was not available. The introduction of distinctive features into the base exemplifies the difficulty. It
was not always possible to label them conclusively as semantic or syntactic. Whereas it was the
original assumption that many aspects of semantics would be assimilated by syntax as they became
better understood, there are those who now believe the opposite to be true – adherents of generative
semantics (GS). From the GS point of view, which is closer to our own, what is generally understood
as syntax (underlying lexical representations) is merely a reflection of yet deeper semantic representations. I have identified this as Level II and called it syntacto-semantic, since it entails the organization
of semantic atoms into semantic molecules, as it were. Ultimately, we relate this process to the referential act and our conception of the part it plays in our ability to communicate (Chapter 7).

SOME OR ALL

Recall that nominal scope is the essential difference between restrictives and non-restrictives. As Jacobs and Rosenbaum point out, the restrictive refers to a subset of professors, i.e. just to *some* of them; whereas the nonrestrictive is inclusive of *all* professors. Referential scope is semantically significant. Therefore, it must be present in the deep structure and cannot be disturbed by transformations. It follows, then, that a quantifier governing scope of reference must be present in the underlying representation of the sentences in question: namely, *some* accompanies *professors* in the restrictive, while *all* accompanies *professors* in the nonrestrictive. We propose, therefore, that the correct rendition of the restrictive matrix is not

> *"professors are idealistic"

but

> "*some* professors are idealistic."

Correspondingly, the unabbreviated version of the nonrestrictive matrix is

> "*all* professors are idealistic."

Notice that *all* does not alter the semantic interpretation of either the relative or the conjoined versions:

> "(all) professors are idealistic and they enjoy poetry"
> "(all) professors, who enjoy poetry, are idealistic."

This is further evidence that *all* is present in the deep structure – it is understood whether it actually appears in the surface structure or not.

Further justification for positing *some* and *all* as abstract quantifiers in the deep structure is provided by another interesting sentence type. Compound sentences involving 'some-other' dichotomies are common:

> (8a) Professors who enjoy poetry are idealistic, but other professors aren't.

Whenever a compound using *other* is possible, it is clear that the scope of the head noun is less than comprehensive. If *all* is used or understood in the head noun, no 'other' compound is possible:

> *"Professors, who enjoy poetry, are idealistic, but other professors aren't."

Thus, if a sentence with *other* can be constructed, the quantifier in the head noun must be *some*: if such a sentence is ungrammatical, the quantifier in the head noun must be *all*. This corresponds to the mutually exclusive distribution of *some–others* and *all – none*.

We are now prepared to construct a conjoined paraphrase of the restrictive relative clause:

"some professors are idealistic and *they* enjoy poetry."

This sentence is difficult to differentiate semantically from:

"professors who enjoy poetry are idealistic."

In each case just those professors who are idealistic enjoy poetry. The same allegations are made about the same subset of professors. The following sentence does entail a semantic difference, however:

*"sóme [stressed] professors who enjoy poetry are idealistic."

We star the sentence because it deviates semantically from the interpretation we require. It employs an overt quantifier, which, similar to cardinals in general, readily accepts prepositional modifiers:

"sóme of the professors who enjoy poetry are idealistic."
"five of the professors who enjoy poetry are idealistic."

In order to obtain the semantic interpretation we require, the underlying element *some* must either be encliticized (de-stressed), or deleted if the antecedent noun is to occur with a restrictive modifier in the surface structure. Otherwise, the semantic reading becomes *some of some*, a subset of a subset of professors. This suggests that the abstract quantifier we have called *some* may be phonologically realized in either of two ways: (1) as close-juncture (suppressed juncture) between the head noun and the clause; or (2) articulation of the quantifier *sóme*. If both are used, then compounded quantifiers are understood to be present in the deep structure: *some of some*. This leads to the most interesting possibility of all – it should be possible to get a nonrestrictive paraphrase of a restrictive by retaining *sóme* and not using close-juncture. This is in fact the case:

"sóme professors, who enjoy poetry, are idealistic"[15]
(of professors, some, who are idealistic, enjoy poetry).

On the basis of these observations, the restrictive-nonrestrictive distinction appears reducible to the following selectional options:

$$\left\{ \begin{array}{l} \textit{SOME} \; + \; \text{Juncture} \\ \left\{ \begin{array}{l} \textit{Some} \\ \emptyset \end{array} \right\} + \; \text{Suppressed Juncture} \end{array} \right\}$$

where *SOME* is the overt quantifier, and *Some* is an enclitic article (indefinite).

---

[15]   Note that the sentence is ambiguous, depending on whether the relative clause is construed to modify *some* or *professors*. The reading we have in mind is provided in parentheses.

It is not our intent to discuss here the inadequacies of the above proposal, or the problems and questions which it raises. The point we wish to make is that the criterion of semantic identity is sufficiently elusive to make it difficult to apply. To employ it as the basis for crucial arguments without a formal means of making semantic evaluations entails a calculated risk.

The reader may have noticed that the direction of the foregoing analysis has led to a rather embarrassing impasse.

We now have a restrictive, a nonrestrictive, and a conjoined version of the original example sentence which appear to be semantically equivalent:

> "professors who enjoy poetry are idealistic"
> "sóme professors, who enjoy poetry, are idealistic"
> "sóme professors are idealistic, and they enjoy poetry."

Further support for the argument that these sentences are semantically equivalent, at least so far as the scope of referents is concerned, is provided by the grammatical occurrence of *other* in sentences conjoined to each of them:

> "professors who enjoy poetry are idealistic, but other professors aren't"
> "of professors, some, who enjoy poetry, are idealistic, but other professors aren't"
> "some professors are idealistic, and they enjoy poetry, but other professors aren't."

Whereas semantic equivalence between conjoined structures and nonrestrictive relatives was originally cited as evidence for the conjoined-structure origin of nonrestrictives, we now are faced with a restrictive, a nonrestrictive, and a conjoined structure which are semantically equivalent to the extent, at least, that in each case the same set of referents is understood to be idealistic and to enjoy poetry.

Thus, arguments similar to those put forward to justify the derivation of nonrestrictives from conjoined sentences can be used to conclude that all of the types in question come from the same deep structure origin. In fact, it would seem just as plausible to derive conjoined sentences from relative clauses, assuming that the restrictive-nonrestrictive distinction is solely a reflection of referential quantification – *ALL* or *SOME*. Perhaps the popular idea that restrictive clauses cannot be removed without changing the meaning of the matrix sentence is an illusion arising from considering surface structure only and stems from failure to recast the sentence properly – *SOME* must be supplied since the option of applying close juncture is denied.

THE COUNTER-PROPOSAL

We shall not derive conjoined sentences from relative clauses, or vice versa, but assume that the underlying structure of all relative clauses is that which we have proposed (See Figure 2.5), conjunction being a distinct and autonomous operation.

Thus we reiterate our assumption that language-specific rules of grammar interpret and reflect syntacto-semantic deep structures, yielding a lexical representation, BUT DO NOT DISTURB OR ALTER STRUCTURAL RELATIONSHIPS, WHICH WE TAKE TO BE AN ESSENTIAL INGREDIENT OF MEANING.

Although we shall cite evidence to support the validity of our assumptions, there are also methodological reasons for adopting them. By assuming that structure is one ingredient of meaning, we shall be forced to evaluate the semantic value of grammatical relations more carefully. Moreover, such an approach forces the investigation of alternative mechanisms for generating structure. Although we may hesitate to deviate from the transformational 'frame-of-mind' to which we have become accustomed, the theoretical difficulties confronting us bear witness of the need for innovations.

Alternative proposals will now be made for dealing with the restrictive-nonrestrictive dichotomy within the revised theoretical framework we have elaborated thus far. It will be argued that all types of relative clauses have the phrase structure we have described, but differ in certain values deriving from the referential (rather than structural) status of the antecedent. As a preliminary step we shall present our views on the nature and origin of syntacto-semantic features and how they relate to the theoretical framework of this study.

SUBCATEGORIZATION

Initial approaches to the problem of subcategorization were defective in some respects.[16] It was first noted that rewrite rules of the form $N \rightarrow \left\{ \begin{array}{l} \text{Common} \\ \text{Proper} \end{array} \right\}$ were inappropriate. Subsequent analyses made use of binary distinctive features, adopting the theory and formal conventions from phonology.[17] Weaknesses of rewrite rules were thus overcome, but other problems were quickly recognized. The feature system failed to differentiate between semantic and syntactic features. Moreover, attempts to explicate co-occurrence by formalizing selectional restrictions (in terms of distinctive features specified on lexical entries) has recently come under attack by McCawley, who argues that selectional restrictions are not imposed by a lexical item but by presuppositions about the referents of those constituents.[18] McCawley further asserts that discussions to date leave the mistaken impression that a relatively small number of very general features are involved, such as $\{\pm \text{Humans}\}$, $\{\pm \text{Animate}\}$, etc., which are syntactic insofar as they participate in the application of syntactic rules. The essence of McCawley's position on the matter is that selectional restrictions are actually semantic in nature. Moreover, the full range of properties that figure in semantic representation can impose selectional restrictions. Thus, McCawley argues

[16]   Chomsky, 1965, 79.
[17]   Chomsky, 1965.
[18]   McCawley, 1968.

that it is the semantic interpretation of an entire syntactic constituent such as a noun phrase that determines whether a selectional restriction is met or violated.

Evidence to support these arguments is abundant. He offers, for example, sentences such as:

> (9a) My neighbor hurt himself.
> (9b) My neighbor hurt herself.
> (9c) My arm is bleeding.
> (9d) *The statue's arm is bleeding.

Presupposition as to the sex of the referent of *neighbor* clarifies the form of the reflexive pronoun in (9a) and (9b). Otherwise, all human nouns would have to be further subcategorized by the rule: $\{+\text{Human}\} \rightarrow \{\pm \text{Female}\}$. Sentence (9d) is semantically anomalous because of the presupposition that the intended referent is inanimate and cannot bleed, although it does have an arm.[19]

As relating to the form of lexical entries, let us further elucidate how such an entry must be interpreted. As is well known, *who* normally has a human referent in standard English. But observe the relative pronouns in the following sentence:

> (10a) The lexical entry *boy*, which is $\{+\text{Human}\}$, takes the relative pronoun *which* in this sentence rather than *who*.

The apparent contradiction is easily resolved by noting that the assertion made by the relative clause about *boy* is false: *boy* is not $\{+\text{Human}\}$. It is $\{-\text{Human}\}$. If we are to be explicit, we will not say that a lexical entry is specified $\{\pm \text{Human}\}$, but that it is specified as designating referents which are typically presupposed to be $\{\pm \text{Human}\}$.

The 'chameleon'-like disposition of words in referential context is easily illustrated by sentences such as:

> (11a) Fido, *who* is my dog, likes cheese.
> (11b) Fido, *which* is my dog, likes cheese.
> (11c) The dirty dog *who* did that will pay!

These data lend credence to the familiar assertion that words are not meaningful in and of themselves, but only indirectly through a referent. As noted, *boy* is not $\{\pm \text{Human}\}$, but rather the class of referents which the lexeme typically refers to is $\{+\text{Human}\}$. Notice, however, that the referent of Fido in (11a) is not human, but is nevertheless perceived to be a person, as the relative pronoun *who* clearly indicates. In sentence (11c) *dog* denotes a non-typical referent (token-odd), namely a human being. The noun reflects certain presupposed properties of the intended referent (as *who* clearly indicates) while simultaneously imputing the presence of other properties in the referent by association with the typical referent class of the lexeme, namely dogs.

---

[19]   McCawley, 1968.

It is obvious that the sentences discussed above are neither rare nor ungrammatical. A decision to exclude them as irrelevant examples of performance would be unfortunate, since an analysis which explicates their behavior is equally relevant to a correct statement of lexical structure and selectional restrictions.[20]

In summary, we adopt the following position with regard to distinctive features, lexemes, and selectional restrictions:

(1) Lexemes reflect presupposed properties of referents rather than having a specified matrix of immutable inherent features.

(2) Selectional restrictions are imposed on other constituents by the presupposed properties of a referent, not by the lexical entry per se.

Before proceeding, it seems appropriate to attempt a formalization of the process underlying (1) above. Let L denote the lexeme and U a set of potential referents for L (the universe of L). The symbols l and r correspond respectively to L as a token and to U as the particular referent of l selected from U:

$$U/L \rightarrow \quad r \quad / \quad l$$
$$\begin{bmatrix} \alpha & a \\ \beta & b \\ \gamma & c \end{bmatrix} \begin{bmatrix} \alpha & a \\ \beta & b \\ \gamma & c \end{bmatrix}$$

The relationship of lexeme to referent is shown here in its most general form.

The formalization resembles grammatical rules of agreement in that feature specifications in l have their origin in r, which corresponds to Level II in the strata of linguistic representations (see page 16). Lower case a, b, c, ... are possible semantic features. The Greek letters are variable over the values + and −. Variable specifications convert to + or − by virtue of their presence or absence in the referent.

The above formula expresses the lexical relationship in its most general form. It is assumed that blocks of rules of the type illustrated in Appendix I implement lexical realization, since word order and placement of affixes must also be accounted for.

---

[20]   I must admit that certain reservations lurk in my mind with respect to COMPETENCE and PERFORMANCE and their application to linguistic research. Others apparently have similar misgivings. Robert Binnick, for example, notes "that performance has merely been a catch-all term used by linguists with a lot of nasty facts on their hands they had no way of handling." (Binnick, 1969, 26). I suspect that language may turn out to be so thoroughly permeated by phenomena now relegated to the realm of performance that their exclusion would reduce the range of linguistic data available for models of competence to ridiculous proportions. It is appropriate, perhaps, to note that the alleged discrepancy between syntactic structure and phonological phrasing mentioned above is considered seriously as a matter not belonging "to grammar – to the theory of competence – at all." (Chomsky and Halle, 1968, 372). There is a real danger, I believe, that crucial evidence may be overlooked or disregarded if the competence-performance criterion is applied too loosely.

$$r + r' = U$$

We propose that in order to fully describe the structure of reference it is not sufficient to consider the scope or cardinality of r alone.[21] The *some-other* patterns examined above indicate that possible referents not included by r in a particular instance are just as relevant to semantic interpretation as those which are included. Let us stipulate that the referential value corresponding to *some* is r, and that the value underlying *other(s)* is r'. Taken together, we shall say that they constitute the Universe (U) of a lexeme participating in an utterance. Since we are obviously dealing with sets of referents, possible or realized, we define these values in set terminology. r and r' are disjoint, i.e. r' is the complement of r. If r' is not empty, *other(s)* may occur, since U has not been exhausted by r. A restricted referential posture exists for r when r' is not empty. If r is nonrestricted, then r' has no elements to be denoted by *other(s)*, r being equal to U.

The above remarks are simply a restatement of certain longstanding assumptions, namely, that human perception of environmental phenomena is in terms of types and individuals. Common nouns generally denote perceptual types; proper nouns generally denote individuals. For example, the word *boy* does not have a unique referent, unless employed generically, or unless nonrestrictivization has occurred. The value of r for proper nouns is fixed, however, unless a special context arises to alter the original situation: *The John I know lives on Healey*.

The claim advanced is, in essence, that every nominal (actually, every lexeme) in an utterance has two semantically relevant values – r and r'. The restrictive-nonrestrictive distinction is solely a function of these, having nothing whatsoever to do with phrase structure. If $r' = \emptyset$, reference is nonrestricted; if $r' \neq \emptyset$, r is restricted. Relative clauses are simply reflective of this aspect of referential structure. If restrictedness is considered from the point of view of these values, the 'duality' implied by restrictive constructions resolves itself naturally – r' as well as r figures in semantic interpretation. *Eleven apostles were faithful, but the other betrayed his Master*.

An extensive examination of relative clause constructions suggests that any and all such structures can be explicated in terms of the relationships we have defined. Whereas a taxonomic approach might lead one to set up lists of word-types occurring

---

[21]   It is interesting to note that the analysis presented in the following paragraphs, although arrived at independently, corresponds in essence with the analysis of relative clauses presented in the Port-Royal *Logic*: "A complex expression is a mere *explication* [nonrestrictive clause] if either (1) the idea expressed by the complex expression is already contained in the comprehension of the idea or (2) some accidental characteristic of all the inferiors of an idea is expressed by the principal word. ... A complex expression is a *determination* [restrictive clause] if the extension of the idea expressed by the complex term is less than the extension of the idea expressed by the principal word" (pp. 59–60 as quoted in Chomsky, 1966, 36). We refer to the extension of the "idea expressed by the principal word" as U; and to "the extension of the idea expressed by the complex term" as r. r' represents any difference between the extension of the word and the extension of the complex term.

most naturally with nonrestrictive clauses (proper nouns, noncount nouns, generic nouns, italicized words, nouns with demonstratives, etc.), each of these categories can also occur with restrictives in the proper context. A very general taxonomy can be achieved if nonrestrictive categories are reduced to all-inclusive, and uniquely singular or plural (*dogs*, *John*, and *The Beatles*, respectively). Even this taxonomy reduces to the single relationship we have defined, however: Either a singular or plural value for r is all-inclusive if r' is empty. Thus one simple formula can be used for any relative:

If $r = U$, r' is empty and the relative is nonrestrictive;
if $r \neq U$, r' is not empty and the relative is restrictive.

In any case, however, the union of r and r' must equal U:

"Of the twelve apostles eleven were faithful, but the other one wasn't"
*"Eleven of the apostles were faithful, but the other apostles weren't"

Violation of this principle leads to semantic anomaly, as in the second sentence above.

RESTRICTIVE OR RESTRICTED

It has been generally assumed that restrictive clauses actually restrict referential scope, as their name implies, but this point of view needs clarification in order to be compatible with the theoretical framework of this study. We have argued that the restrictive-nonrestrictive distinction does not derive from different phrase structures, but from the referential values r, r' and U. If this is the case, one would expect the distinction to be more general, i.e. not confined to nouns with overt relative clauses.[22] That such is the case is evidenced by sentences such as the following:

(12a) I bought a cottage, but the chimney___needs repair.
(12b) The car___belongs to Jim.
(12c) A friend___surprised me with a visit yesterday.
(12d) The first men to land on the moon___*were* Americans.
(12e) The dog___is man's best friend.
(12f) He hit me in the stomach___.
(12g) Zero (0)___is less than one (1).

The reader is to construct for himself relative clauses for the nominals followed by a blank. It will be noted that the selection of a restrictive or a nonrestrictive modifier for these is by no means an arbitrary choice. In each case one feels constrained by context to select one over the other. Generally the selections for this set are: a. nonrestrictive; b. restrictive; c. restrictive; d. nonrestrictive; e. nonrestrictive; f. nonrestrictive; g. nonrestrictive. Although it is possible to imagine a context, perhaps,

---

[22] See Bach, 1968, for another approach to the phenomenon we are attempting to describe.

where (12 a-g) could occur with the opposite type relative clause without doing violence to their semantic interpretation, such a switch may presuppose a referential status at odds with reality or conventional usage. For example, in (f) a restrictive clause would imply that I have more than one stomach, while a restrictive clause in (e) would alter the essence of a popular saying.

From the foregoing it emerges that the terminology (restrictive-nonrestrictive) applied to relative clauses is not entirely adequate. The terms suggest that it is the act of constructing a particular type of modifier which determines referential scope, while the evidence indicates that words are restricted or nonrestricted in their referential scope independently of overt modifiers. In other words, the posture of a relative clause is not DETERMINATIVE of the status of reference, but only REFLECTIVE of it.

Viewing the matter from a slightly different angle, a relative clause may be restricted in the authenticity of its predication to a proper subset of U, there being elements in U for which the predication does not hold. From the speaker's point of view a particular referent is RESTRICTED or NONRESTRICTED with regard to the universe of a given word or phrase. This is simply reflected by the type of juncture selected for overt relative modifiers. From the hearer's point of view, juncture serves as a cue to how the intended referent is analysed by the speaker. Thus, it is from the hearer's point of view that a relative clause can be said to be restrictive or nonrestrictive, since it is he who must abstract from the posture of the relative whether the intended referent is to be construed as equal or unequal to the universe of the antecedent.

We have thus far sought to support the claim that the restrictive-nonrestrictive distinction in relative clauses does not derive from differences in underlying phrase structure, but from lexico-referential relationships definable in terms of r, r', and U. These relationships have been referred to as the status of reference. Evidence has been cited to demonstrate that status of reference is reflected by modifiers, not determined by them. We now return to the nature of features and the manner of their specification.

THE SPECIFICATION OF r, r', AND U

Consider sentences of the following type:

> (13a) *Two Musketeers escaped but the other Musketeers didn't.
> (13b) *Eleven apostles were faithful but the other apostles weren't.
> (13c) *My wife who is thrifty buys skim milk.
> (13d) *My nose which was unprotected got frost-bitten.
> (13e) *Dogs which are carnivorous eat meat.

There is nothing superficially deviant in the grammatical structure of these sentences, yet they are all semantically anomalous. The restrictions violated have to do precisely with certain presuppositions we make about referents. Thus, it is presupposed that there are only three Musketeers, only twelve apostles, only one wife, only one nose, and that the number of non-carnivorous dogs is zero. In fact, the relative values of r, r', and U are presupposed in precisely the same sense as those discussed by McCawley. It follows then, that the specification of these features is a part of the same interpretive function expressed by the general lexical rule (p. 44).

Thus far, the discussion of referential status has been based on relative clauses. In subsequent chapters we will indicate how $r + r' = U$ is operative for modifiers of all kinds, including adjectives, adverbs, prepositional phrases, etc. The behavior of r, r', and U in modifier sequences will also be considered.

3

THE AUTONOMY OF CONJUNCTION VS. SUBJUNCTION

In the preceding chapter it was seen that a problem arises in accounting for the distribution of envelope features (e.g. the interrogative), if relative clauses are derived from conjoined sentences.[1] Other significant problems also arise if a generalized transformation of this sort is permitted. For example, proponents of the conjoined sentence hypothesis for nonrestrictives must take into consideration certain constraints governing the compatibility of conjoined sentences, such as sequential harmony. The assertion that nonrestrictives derive from conjoined sentences seems to imply that any nonrestricted clause might just as easily occur as a conjoined sentence. This does not appear to be the case, however:

(1a) A bomb, which exploded, killed twenty people.
(1b) A bomb killed twenty people and it exploded.

(1c) John, who read the book for the first time, liked it very much.
(1d) John liked the book very much and he read it for the first time.

(1e) The Titanic, which set out on her maiden voyage, sank.
(1f) The Titanic sank and she set out on her maiden voyage.

(1g) John, who took the exam Saturday, failed it.
(1h) John failed the exam and he took it Saturday.

(1i) The Cagers, who will be tops this year, lost all their games last year.
(1j) The Cagers lost all their games last year and they will be tops this year.

(1k) The plane, which was last seen a week ago, turned up today.
(1l) The plane turned up today and it was last seen a week ago.

(1m) My grandfather, who was called to the ministry, swore once.
(1n) My grandfather swore once and he was called to the ministry.

(1o) Kailem, who failed his first exam, eventually became a scholar.
(1p) Kailem eventually became a scholar and he failed his first exam.

---

[1] See pp. 33–35.

(1q) New York City, which is extremely large, has millions of people.
(1r) New York City has millions of people and it is extremely large.

Some of the above can be improved by using perfect tenses or intonation to clarify sequential relationships or by inverting the order of the clauses, but the semantic anomalies which occur in the conjoined versions arise in general as a result of the incompatibility of the constituent sentences in a conjoined relationship.

Examples of the above sort are legion. The defect might possibly be overcome by claiming that conjoined sentences not meeting certain constraints obligatorily become relative clauses, but this is not entirely convincing.

There is still a more compelling reason to exclude conjoined structures as a source for *all* relative clauses. We have seen that in a sequence of restricted clauses, each successive relative pronoun takes as its antecedent the head noun as modified by preceding relatives in the sequence. In terms of the values r, r', and U, the situation in a restricted sequence is the following: r remains constant (the referent remains the same), but U (and hence r') becomes increasingly diminished. The sequence terminates with unique identification of the referent for the hearer, such that $r' = \emptyset$, as is clearly the case in the following sentence:

(2) Men who are wealthy who are generous, who are few indeed, are a
    blessing to society.

Thus, there are understood to be other men than those who are wealthy; men who are wealthy but not generous; but of those who are wealthy, the generous ones are a blessing to society. The universe for *who*[1] is men; U for *who*[2] is *men who are wealthy;* etc. Referential values for a restricted sequence align themselves as shown in Figure 3.1. It is not clear how the structural relationships of modifiers in such a sequence could be handled in terms of conjunction, considering the manner in which modifiers overlap each other.

The phenomena of nonrestrictivization discussed earlier is clearly related to the diminution of r'. Whether an overt relative sequence occurs or not, r' reduces to $\emptyset$ during a single act of reference. Nonrestrictivization, i.e. the act of reference, is not completed until $r' = \emptyset$.

One might argue (in order to retain the concept of multiple occurrences of the head noun in the super- and subordinate sentences[2]) that r diminishes and hence nonrestrictivization does not occur immediately (no value for r being used more than once). This, however, is counter-intuitive as well as untenable – if r has a singular value in the first term of the sequence, how can it possibly diminish?

(3a) The boy sitting at the table whom we saw ....

---

[2]   See p. 24, Figure 2.1.

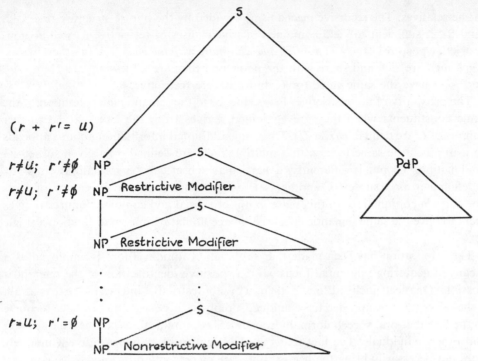

Fig. 3.1. The values of r and r' for a given antecedent determine whether the modifier will be restrictive or nonrestrictive.

The autonomous nature of subjunction is likewise apparent if adjectives are considered. *Generous wealthy men...* is quite distinct from *Generous and wealthy men....* The latter expression is equivalent to *Men who are generous and wealthy...*, which involves conjoined rather than subjoined adjectives. The conjoined elements do not imply that either class of men is a subset of the other. This is not true of the relationships defined by the adjective sequence, however. *Blue white shirts* is semantically deviant; *blue and white shirts* is not.

It is appropriate at this point to comment on the properties of nonrestrictive relative sequences, structures which, because of their referential status, do exhibit characteristics somewhat akin to conjoined sentences.

It is somewhat unnatural to construct a sequence of nonrestrictive clauses, since if $r = U$, no further specialization is possible in terms of subsets. Such constructions are quite acceptable, however, with one relative occurring as a nonrestrictive adjective: *The industrious Chinese, who work unceasingly, are prospering.* The sequential relative version is rather more cumbersome: *The Chinese, who are industrious, who work very hard, are prospering.*

The tendency in nonrestrictives is to conjoin them, so that serial facts are reported about the referent: *The Chinese, who are industrious, and who work very hard, are prospering.* We cannot, however, take this as evidence for a conjoined sentence origin of the relatives. The recursive mechanism provided by the phrase structure rule $S \to S$ (and $S)_1^n$ is sufficient to yield conjoined relative clauses of restrictive as well as non-restrictive posture: *Men who are rich and who share with the poor* . . . . In other, words, some men are rich and share with the poor, and they are a blessing. . . . Here *who*[1] and *who*[2] have the same value for U, but both are restrictive.

The proximity of nonrestrictives in a sequence to the semantic interpretation of the same constituents when they are conjoined derives from the fact that no further subsets of U are definable ($r = U$). Thus, any additional information about r appends to it in much the same fashion that multiple facts are defined on a given subset via conjunction. To put it differently, a particular subset can be specialized either by redefining it as a subset of another set, or by constructing an inventory of facts about it via conjunction. In this sense, both sequential and conjoined nonrestrictives seem to have the same semantic effect, i.e. of accumulating information upon a single set.

The implication has been made that subjunction (modification) is employed as a means of acquiring referential focus, so that positive identification of the referent is possible. One feels inclined to ask, then, why nonrestrictive intersection exists at all, if the referent is presupposed to be unique. A reply to this question must have recourse to the fact that oral speech normally constitutes communication between the speaker and other individuals. The fact that the speaker identifies a given referent uniquely does not necessarily bring the hearer to a state of perception or knowledge equal to the speaker's. In fact, the referent may be entirely unknown to the hearer. Subjunction in this case provides a structure for reporting relevant information about the referent without being bound by constraints which govern the conjunctability of sentences.

There is another reason for questioning a transformation which derives relative clauses from conjoined sentences. Noun phrase relatives are only one type of clausal modifier. As the discussion proceeds, we shall identify clauses with adjectival, adverbial, verbal, predicate phrase, and even sentence antecedents.[3] Of these, the latter three appear to be inherently nonrestrictive, while the others may be, depending upon the referential status of the antecedent. Those who adopt the conjoined-origin hypothesis for noun phrase relatives would, for the sake of consistency and generality, need to derive all of these from conjoined sentences. Moreover, phrasal modifiers, which may also be restrictive or nonrestrictive, appear to be instances of the same structure as relative clauses.[4] Assuming that this is the case, sentence modifiers, among others, would derive from conjuncts. But it is not at all clear what sort of conjuncts modifiers like *of course*, *indeed*, etc., might be derived from.

In short, a generalization of the transformation proposed to derive relative clauses from conjuncts results in rather serious difficulties. Since the semantic arguments advanced to support such an approach are inconclusive, it seems necessary to investi-

[3]　Examples are cited in Appendix II, as well as in the text.
[4]　See Chapter 6.

gate other alternatives. In particular, rather than generalize the proposed transformation, we have reformulated the relative clause rule,[5] which we shall ultimately generalize to account for all subordinate structures. The distinction between restrictive and nonrestrictive modifiers will be dealt with in terms of r, r', and U.

INTERROGATIVE SHIFT

Subjoined structures, as noted above,[6] tend to remain declarative regardless of the modality of the superordinate sentence, whereas conjoined sentences appear to share in the modality imposed upon the compounded structure in which they participate. Although there are structures rather difficult to analyze in this respect, it is usually possible to test for con- versus subjunction by observing the distribution of the interrogative envelope. This discovery procedure we shall refer to as the INTERROGATIVE-SHIFT TEST (IST). Applying IST to the following sentences, one can conclude that sentences (6)-(9) contain subjoined structures, but that (10)-(11) involve conjunction.

(6)   The apple you ate had a worm in it.
(6a) Did the apple *that you ate* have a worm in it?

(7)   Pearls are as valuable as diamonds are.
(7a) Are pearls as valuable *as diamonds are?*

(8)   Jim must learn by experience, like everyone else (does).
(8a) Must Jim learn by experience, *like everyone* else (does)?

(9)   The Smiths have a dog like ours (is).
(9a) Do the Smiths have a dog *like ours* (is)?

(10)   Mary washed the dishes and Jan dried them.
(10a) Did Mary wash the dishes and Jan dry them?

(11)   We have a Plymouth, but Mike has a Ford.
(11a) Do we have a Plymouth, but Mike a Ford?

Notice the italicized clauses. In spite of the interrogative enveloping the matrix, the subjoined clauses retain their declarative modality. Interrogative shift includes all clauses CONJOINED on the same level, however, as the latter two sentence pairs demonstrate. Generally speaking, IST is a dependable discovery procedure, and we shall use it in our analysis.

---

[5]   Chapter 2, p. 28.
[6]   See p. 34.

4

HOMOGENEOUS SUBJUNCTION

X/X S

We must now acknowledge the implications of the foregoing analysis of relative clauses for other grammatical constituents. Since we have admitted NP/NP S as a rule of grammar, there is no *a priori* reason to suppose that similar rules do not subordinate S to constituents other than NP. One might expect that NP/NP S is a particular instance of a more general structural relationship X/X S, where X is any major lexical category. An immediate effect of such a generalization would be the elimination of 'embedding' transformations – if subordinate structures are generated intact, there is no need of any rule to transpose them from some other position in the sentence. This effect is not unexpected, however. As noted above, a similar effect was noted by Chomsky as a consequence of investing the phrase structure rules with S-recursive power. It is, in fact, an axiom of linguistic theory that modification of one component is immediately reflected elsewhere in the grammar.

A search for structures corresponding to the generalized formula for subjunction seems to confirm occurrences of the following particular instances of it in addition to

NP/NP S:

      PdP/PdP S
      VP/VP S
      AdjP/AdjP S
      AdvP/AdvP S
      QP/QP S (Q = quantifier)

PdP/PdP S

These structures are as common and natural as NP relatives. Some ambiguity results from the fact that the relative pro-form *like* (*as*) may have adjectival, adverbial, and verbal antecedents (to be discussed shortly) as well as predicate phrase antecedents. The modificational effect of PdP/PdP S is straightforward: x does what y does.

(1a) Phil worked overtime Saturday, like (as) Buz (did).

Predicate phrase relative clauses are often preposed:

(1b) Like Buz, Phil worked overtime Saturday.

Interrogative shift passes them by, thus revealing their subordinated relationship to the main clause:

(1c) Did Phil work overtime Saturday, like Buz?

The PdP as a whole is perceived as a unique referent ($r' = \emptyset$), so that these clauses are nonrestrictive. A phrase marker for predicate phrase relatives is given in Figure 4.1.

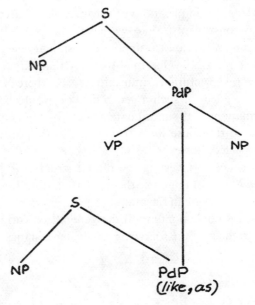

Fig. 4.1. The structure of predicate phrase relative clauses (PdP/PdP S).

VP/VP S

It appears possible for intersection to occur on VP, excluding the direct object,

(2a) I fristicized the seropulus, like (as) you did the relampicule.

the essence of which is *I did to x what you did to y*. IST indicates that clauses of this type are subordinate. Figure 4.2 illustrates the structure of VP/VP S.

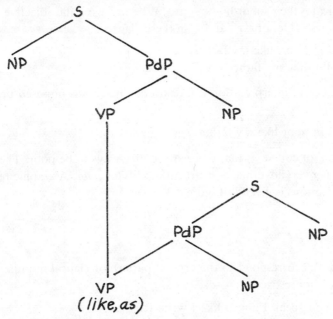

Fig. 4.2. The structure of verb phrase relative clauses (VP/VP S).

AdjP/AdjP S

Our range of expression would be seriously curtailed if these did not occur: *I want to be like father was, We have a car like yours*, etc. It is convenient to be able to say that "x is like y", thus focusing upon or implying an attribute of someone or some-

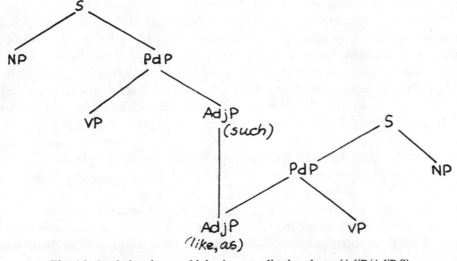

Fig. 4.3. A relative clause subjoined to an adjective phrase (AdjP/AdjP S).

thing. IST indicates their subordinate status. Whether a specific adjective is mentioned or not determines values of r, r', and U in these clauses:

(3a) I'm poor, like my father was.
(3b) I'm like my father was.

Notice the change of interpretation if a restrictive pattern is imposed upon a specific adjective:

(3c) I'm poor like my father was.

The implication, of course, is that there are sundry ways to be poor. The intersection has shifted to a covert adverbial constituent modifying *poor*. A graphic representation of these constructions is given in Figure 4.3.

AdvP/AdvP S

Adverbial relatives correspond to the general pattern of clausal modifiers. They may be restrictive or nonrestrictive:

(4a) You speak Finnish like I write Russian.
(4b) You speak Finnish haltingly, like I write Russian.

The reader may apply IST for himself to verify the subordinate status of adverbial relatives.

There are other constructions corresponding to the morphological contour of adverbial modifiers which are more difficult to analyze: *Uncle Tom sells shoes, like Daddy works at the office*. Although sentences like this strike one as being of marginal grammaticality, they are not uncommon in colloquial speech. Their peculiarity stems from the lack of any apparent antecedent in the main clause. The implication of such sentences is simply that both events occur, which suggests the possibility of constructing a covert adverbial of affirmation (or negation) as the shared constituent. Sentences such as the following lend evidence for this approach: *I'm talented like you're a prima donna*! It is implied, of course, that neither is the case.

The foregoing remarks are made under the assumption that adverbs are a legitimate category, i.e. not reducible to combinations of other prime categories (such as those which constitute prepositional phrases, for example). Other linguists have recognized that restrictive clauses introduced by the five W's and H (who, where, what, when, why, and how) are relatives, but were obliged to embed them all to NP's in prepositional phrases via the rule NP → NP S, since no other non-transformational vehicle was available to perform the embedding. For the moment we do not care to argue either that adverbs are derivative or that they are not. The generality of the embedding formula we have provided is adequate, however, should this question be decided in favor of adverbs, to subordinate such structures to a constituent labelled AdvP. An illustrative adverbial relative appears in Figure 4.4.

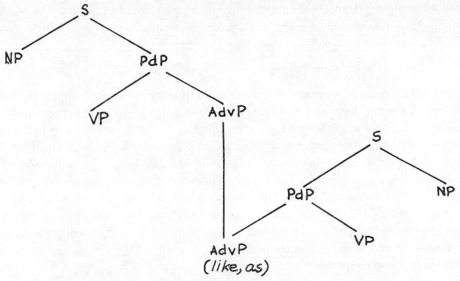

Fig. 4.4. The structure of relative clauses with adverbial antecedents (AdvP/AdvP S).

QP/QP S

It is beyond the scope of this study to discuss comparative constructions in detail. We will, however, propose a schematic analysis suggested by the theory.

Comparative clauses are subordinated, assuming that IST is a valid test. Notice that the clauses following the juncture in the following sentences do not participate in the interrogative:

(5a) Are girls more intelligent than boys are?

The matter of fixing the point of intersection is not so trivial, however. Cursory examination reveals that *be intelligent* is present in both clauses of the example sentence. This we take to be coincidental, since other comparatives share no overt constituent at all:

(5b) She is more beautiful than I am rich.

If, however, we assume that comparatives of equality have the same basic structure as other types, the referential focus can be identified as the quantifying modifier:

(6a) Elephants walk as fast as men can run.
(6b) I sold as many shoes as you bought hats.

What we find in all comparatives is a structure which relates amount, number, or degree of referents used in the super- and subordinate clauses to a covert quantificational base. In this manner relative magnitude is fixed for the referents being compared. Constituents denoting countable referents have cardinality; those which denote non-countable referents have degree, or amount. Thus it is awkward to form a comparative correlating cardinality in one clause with degree in another.

   (7) I'm more intelligent than you have holdings.

Superficially, most comparatives suppress the quantifier constituent, so that no specific number, degree, or base amount is mentioned. It is understood, however, and we shall write it simply as QP (quantifier). QP is used as the basis for comparison in such a way that both constituents undergoing relative quantification are understood to possess it, subject to modifying operations of a mathematical nature – addition (more), subtraction (less), multiplication (x times as). A programmatic structure of comparatives is provided by P rules such as the following: XP → AdvP X; AdvP → M QP; where XP denotes NP, AdjP or AdvP and M subtends mathematical operations of the type referred to above. QP, of course, denotes a base quantity. Thus, QP is made available for intersection as a node independent of M. Figure 4.5 illustrates the structure provided by these proposals.

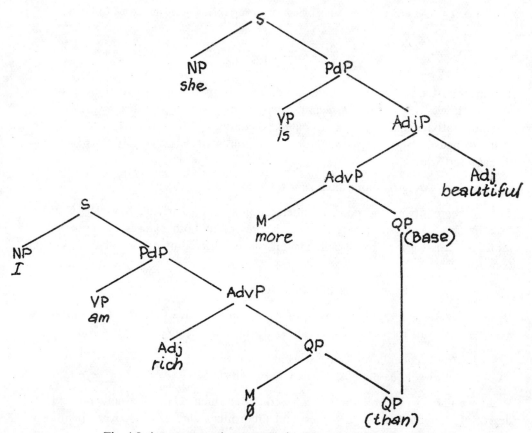

Fig. 4.5. A programmatic representation of comparative structure

The rules given impose an adjunctive relationship between AdvP and X, and also between M and QP. Strictly speaking this is not correct. In Chapter 6 the class of predicators is expanded to include adjectives, adverbs, and prepositions, as well as verbs. The result of that change is to permit the autonomous subordination of adjectives, adverbs, and prepositional phrases to the constituents they modify. Assuming that quantificational adverbs are modifiers, at least $XP \rightarrow AdvP\ X$ would be subsumed under $X/X\ S$ and reformalized accordingly.

The status of QP and M in the overall inventory of linguistic categories requires clarification, a task which we shall not undertake here. A number of approaches are attractive, but further comment at this time would be premature. Our intent has been to demonstrate that comparative constructions are amenable to the theory as presented.

5

HETEROGENEOUS SUBJUNCTION

X/Y S

Whereas the instances of subjunction presented so far have been categorially homogeneous (the constituents involved have functioned in the same lexical category in both the super- and sub-ordinate sentences), abstract sentential constituents, as well as other hybrid (derived) forms, suggest that such is not always the case. By generalizing the formula to X/Y S (where X and Y are not necessarily of the same category), a plausible explanation for the recursive nature of derivational processes, as well as the internal labelled bracketing of many derived forms, can be given.

ABSTRACT SENTENTIAL CONSTITUENTS

That a sentence may function as an NP is evidenced by abstract sentential subjects and objects. Such constituents are NP's externally, but sentences internally: $[\ [S] \ ]$:
$$\begin{array}{cc} & \text{NP} \quad \text{NP} \end{array}$$

(1) It surprised me that you arrived so soon.

The rule which accounts for this pattern is NP/S S, where the first S indicates the portion of the subordinate sentence incorporated into the superordinate NP, and the second S simply represents the subjoined sentence. In this case, of course, the entire sentence is incorporated into the NP. In English, the antecedent of S is generally pronounced as *it*, or *-ing*, if the option for the gerundive nominalization (factive) is selected. An illustrative phrase marker for sentences embedded in NP's is given in Figure 5.1.

Abstract sentential constituents occur with antecedents other than NP. They may occur as adverbials, corresponding to AdvP/S S. Consider, for example, a sentence where an entire subjoined sentence functions as the manner adverbial;

(2a) Dad fixed the door so that it wouldn't slam;

as an adverb denoting cause;

(2b) Dad oiled the hinges because the door was squeaking;

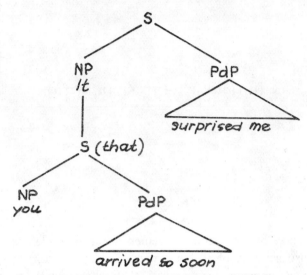

Fig. 5.1. An abstract sentential subject (NP/S S).

or as a time adverbial:

> (2c) We will leave when John has come.

They may likewise function as adjectives: AdjP/S S.

> (3a) I've never seen children such that they didn't like candy.

In fact, this structure corresponds to the expression 'x/x such that...' where x is defined by delineating its properties. Sentential constituents may also function as quantifiers: QP/S S.

> (4a) He was so ill that he couldn't speak.
> (4b) She had so many children that she didn't know what to do.

SENTENCE RELATIVES

Corresponding to the abstract sentential subjects and objects discussed above are structures in which the rank (dependency status) of the participating clauses is reversed. Thus, for NP/S S we have S/NP S. The following pair of sentences exemplifies the correspondence in question:

> (5a) It surprised me that Fred won.
> (5b) Fred won, *which* surprised me.

Sentence (5b) belongs to the class of sentences customarily referred to as sentence relatives. This terminology is suggested by the fact that the antecedent of the relative pronoun (*which*) is not an NP, but an entire sentence (*Fred won* in this case). P-markers for (5a) and (5b) are juxtaposed in Figure 5.2. Notice that heterogeneous subjunction enables us to express the relationship between (5a) and (5b) simply and without transformations.

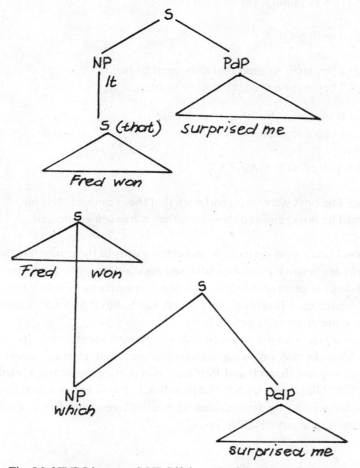

Fig. 5.2. NP/S S becomes S/NP S if the rank of the clauses is reversed.

Another important aspect of the formulation is that the correspondence defined between NP/S S and S/NP S is similarly defined between other pairs of rules. In particular, we have AdvP/S S paired with S/AdvP S;

(6a) We left when John had come.
(6b) John came, *then* we left.

(6c) She fixed the drawer so that it slides easily.
(6d) The drawer slides easily, *like* she fixed it.

(6e) We oiled it because it was rusty.
(6f) It was rusty, *so* we oiled it.

(6g) He went fishing even though it was raining.
(6h) It was raining, *yet* he went fishing.

QP/S S paired with S/QP S;

(7a) They were so tired that they went to bed.
(7b) They went to bed, they were *so* tired.

(7c) It moves so fast that I cannot see it.
(7d) I can't see it, it moves so fast.

and AdjP/S S paired with S/AdjP S:

(8a) The boys were such gentlemen that they removed their hats.
(8b) The boys removed their hats, they were *such* gentlemen.

If the proposed analysis is correct, the italicized words in the examples (*then*, *like*, *so*, *yet*, and *such*) are relative pro-forms with sentence antecedents. In short, the class of sentence relatives is generalized to include many constructions which must otherwise be handled separately.[1] Illustrative P-markers for S/AdvP S, S/QP S, and S/AdjP S configurations are given in Appendix II.

There is no *a priori* reason to assume that only entire sentences may be subjoined heterogeneously. In the following paragraphs we shall examine constructions in English which suggest that VP and PdP may also participate as the Y element of the formula X/Y S. The categories NP, AdjP, and Adv P will be considered as values for X, or, in other words, we shall discuss derivations resulting from nominalization, adjectivalization, and adverbialization.

NP/VP S AND NP/PdP S

Action nominals seem to correspond to NP/VP S. That a verb is embedded in such forms is suggested by the nature of the constituents which cluster about them. In (10a), for example, one can identify sememes corresponding to a complete sentence (10b).

(10a) The sudden firing of the professor by the board provoked a demonstration.
(10b) The board suddenly fired the professor.

[1] Structural inversion and sentence relatives are discussed in some detail in Lytle, 1971.

It will be noted that nominalization of VP alone stimulates certain adjustments in the status of its immediate constituents. In particular, the intuitive subject (*the board*) and the intuitive object (*the professor*) of VP are marked by prepositions (*by* and *of*, respectively), and the logical adverb of manner (*suddenly*) becomes an adjective. These phenomena are apparently the consequence of interposing an NP bracket between VP and its immediate constituents (see Figure 5.3). Although we shall not digress at this point to discuss the adjustments in question as they relate to the theory of junction,[2] we shall indicate how they may be used to advantage in analyzing X/Y S

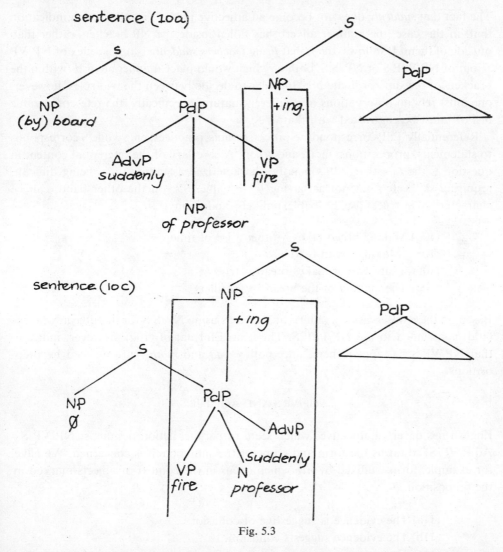

Fig. 5.3

---

[2] Subjunction must be further generalized to encompass phrasal modifiers as well as clausal modifiers if these phenomena are to be handled adequately. See Chapter 6, and the references cited there.

configurations. In essence, the procedure is simply to observe whether constituents in the context of a heterogeneous subjunction (derivational configurations in general) have undergone categorial alternation or have been supplemented by prepositions or case inflections. If they have not, they have fallen within the categorial brackets of the superordinate node. If they have, then they fall outside these brackets.

Consider, for example, the difference between (10a) and (10c).

(10c) Firing teachers suddenly provokes students.

The fact that *suddenly* does not become an adjective in (10c) is taken as an indication that, in this case, the manner adverb has fallen inside the NP brackets rather than outside of them. It follows, then, that *firing teachers suddenly* is not a reflex of NP/VP S, but of NP/PdP S or NP/S S, both of which would place manner adverbs within the brackets of the superordinate NP. In order to decide between the two rules, however, one must rely on observations of a different nature. Specifically, the referential value of PdP must be contrasted with that of S.

Referentially, PdP corresponds to processes, acts, practices, etc., while S corresponds to statements, propositions, facts, and so on. A corollary of the referential content in question is the fact that PdP's may be characterized as taking time, being difficult, requiring skill, etc., but not as having truth value. S's, on the other hand, can be characterized as true, false, probable, unlikely, and so on.

(10d) Making bread takes Mother a lot of time.
(10e) *Making bread is true.
(10f) That Mother makes bread is true.
(10g) The making of the bread by Mother...

Based on these observations, (10f) is analyzed as using NP/S S for its subject, whereas (10d) is assumed to use NP/PdP S. The lexical format of (10g), however, indicates that NP/VP S has applied here, since both *bread* and *mother* are marked by prepositions.

AdjP/VP S AND AdjP/PdP S

English has deverbal adjectives which seem to parallel action nominals (NP/VP S – AdjP/VP S) so far as the form and scope of the subjunction is concerned. We have, for example, forms suffixed by *-ive* which occur in the context of objects marked by the preposition *of*.

(11a) The evidence is suggestive of collusion.
(11b) The evidence suggests collusion.
(11c) The clause is restrictive of the referent.
(11d) The clause restricts the referent.

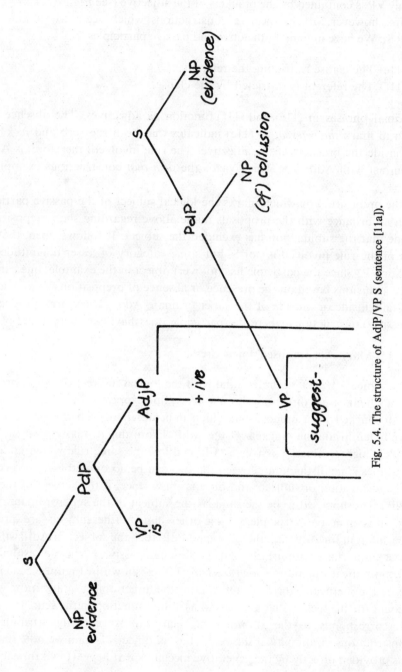

Fig. 5.4. The structure of AdjP/VP S (sentence [11a]).

Assuming that our assumptions regarding the significance of such prepositions are correct, only VP is contained by the brackets of the adjective (see Figure 5.4.).

There are, however, other adjective constructions which seem to subjoin PdP (AdjP/PdP S). We have in mind both active and passive participles.

> (11e) The clause restricting the referent...
>
> (11f) The referent is restricted by the clause.

The participial phrases in (11e) and (11f) function as adjectives. The absence of a preposition to mark *the referent* in (11e) indicates that both the verb and its object (PdP) are inside the brackets of the adjective. The rule involved, therefore, is AdjP/PdP S (contrast with AdjP/S S, which yields the *such that* constructions exemplified by [8a]).

Notice the preposition *by* which marks the logical subject of the passive participle in (11f). In accordance with the proposals made above regarding such prepositions, we conclude that the subjunction has excluded the subject. It follows, then, that the Y element of the rule involved is not S, but some category of lesser magnitude, i.e. either PdP or VP. Since the participle has no overt object in the example, one can not make any conclusions based on the presence or absence of prepositions as to whether the object falls inside or outside of the super-ordinate AdjP. There are, however, in English passive constructions where the participle does have an overt direct object.

> (11g) Mary was promised a new dress.

In (11g) the subject (*Mary*) is coreferential with the logical indirect object of *promise* (*to Mary*) in which case a direct object (*new dress*) does appear. We observe that this object is not marked by a preposition, which indicates that both the verb and the object have fallen inside the brackets of the AdjP. From this it follows that the subjunction rule which produces passives is AdjP/PdP S, the same rule which underlies active participles. The distinction between the two can be accounted for, however, in terms of the disposition of subjects and objects. In essence, if the subject of the embedded PdP is presupposed to be the same as the subject of the superordinate AdjP, then the result is an active participle. On the other hand, if the subjects are presupposed to be different for AdjP and the subjoined PdP, then the subject of AdjP will also be an object somewhere within PdP, and the familiar passive participle results. The two-fold grammatical function of REFERENT in (11f) is shown in Figure 5.5: (1) It is the subject of the predicate adjective, and (2) it is the direct object of RESTRICT, which would account for the feeling that REFERENT has a dual function in the sentence. This, of course, corresponds to the grammatical relationships generally attributed to passive constructions (grammatical subject = logical object)[3]. Again we note that the structure is provided directly by the generative mechanism at Level II. No transforma-

---

[3] See Lytle, 1971, 179–185, for further discussion of passives.

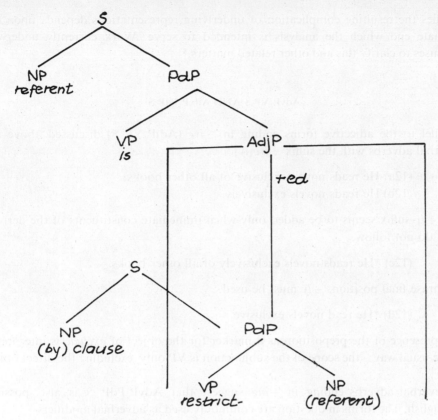

Fig. 5.5. The structure of a passive participle (sentence [11f]).

tion of structure is necessary. The surface structure is provided by lexical interpretation, not by the transformational alteration of underlying structures.

At this point we digress briefly in order to make our theoretical position more explicit. Embeddings are without exception executed by P-rules. Hence, there is no option for deriving adjective participles from any constituent not subtended by an AdjP constituent. There are no transformations to remove it from a node with some other label and embed it in an adjective. It must be generated intact structurally. The only options are those which a language might provide for lexical realization – a process which interprets, but does not alter, underlying constituent relationships.

If we attribute certain internal and external categories to the structure of particular forms, then we must provide for corresponding applications of X/Y S for each labelled constituent. This position entails an extremely strong claim, one which may need to be relaxed somewhat. Notice, for example, that if we adhere to it strictly, prepositional constituents appearing as a consequence of derivation (agentive *by* and obgentive *of*) should be fully accounted for by the Level II representation. Actually, this is not beyond the capability of X/Y S, but whether the explanatory power gained justifies the resulting complication of underlying representations depends upon the ultimate end which the analysis is intended to serve. Work currently underway promises to clarify this and other related matters.[4]

AdvP/VP S AND AdvP/PdP S

Parallel to the adjective forms ending in $+ive$ (AdjP/VP S) discussed above are deverbal adverbs with the suffix $+ive(ly)$.

(12a) He reads novels exclusive of all other books.
(12b) He reads novels exclusively.

The $+ly$ suffix seems to be added only when immediate constituents of the derived form do not follow.

(12c) *He reads novels exclusively of all other books.

In phrase final position, $+ly$ must be used.

(12d) *He read novels exclusive.

The presence of the preposition as a marker for the object of *exclude* is interpreted in the usual way – the scope of the subjunction is VP only, excluding the direct object node.

Deverbal adverbs ending in $+ing$ suggest that AdvP/PdP S is also possible in English. The forms in question are commonly used as adverbial modifiers.

(12e) Seeing a mouse, she screamed.
(12f) He walked along, swinging his cane.

In constructions such as these, the object, when it appears, is not marked by a preposition, which again suggests that PdP rather VP alone has been subjoined (AdvP/PdP S). For some of these constructions it seems possible that the subjunction may be the adverbialization of an entire sentence (*she screamed when/because she saw a mouse*), but for others (12f) Adv/PdP S seems to be the best alternative.

LEXICAL VERSUS STRUCTURAL DERIVATION

We shall refer to the output of heterogeneous subjunction as STRUCTURAL DERIVATIONS. There are, of course, derivational processes which do not fall within this classification. Whereas the suffixes occurring with structurally derived forms have only categorial significance, suffixes on other derived forms have independent semantic

---

[4]   This matter is considered in some detail in Lytle, 1971, 128–137. If pursued to its logical conclusion, the representation of all prepositions at Level II forces a revision of the subjunction formula.

value beyond that of denoting categorial participation. Such suffixes as *-able*, *-ful*, and *-er* are examples of this. When appended to stems, these suffixes result in forms which seem to be the lexical realization of much larger Level II representations. For this reason, we shall refer to them as LEXICAL DERIVATIONS, thus drawing a distinction between them and the reflexes of X/Y S. *Teacher*, for example, denotes someone who teaches, while *reader* can denote either one who reads or a school book (something that one reads). *Destruction* (NP/VP S), on the other hand, does not readily suggest some larger paraphrase. So far as the theoretical context of this study is concerned, lexical derivation may be construed as an abbreviatory process provided by the interpretive grammar of English (the L-rule component of English). It remains to be seen, of course, whether L-rules will be an adequate device for handling semantic phenomena characteristic of lexical derivations. Although it is feasible to formulate L-rules which encode entire fragments of trees as a single derived form, it is not clear whether rules of this kind can be generalized to any significant degree.[5]

We should point out that the approach to derivation presented herein is neither lexicalist nor transformationalist in the sense discussed by Chomsky.[6] Transformational embeddings are supplanted by X/Y S, which operates at Level II. The lexicalist hypothesis advanced by Chomsky, whereby certain lexemes would exercise selective options for lexical category, is not subscribed to, because the level of deep structure utilized by Chomsky for the formulation of the lexical hypothesis seems to be an intermediate one not actually involved in the determination of the relationships in question. It is surely true that lexemes develop features which impose morphological and phonological constraints, but selectional restrictions which are semantically significant are lexically independent – distinct lexical interpretations of the same referential base entail the same selectional restrictions.

---

[5] An alternative to lexical interpretation as presented here is discussed in Lytle, 1971, Chapter IV.
[6] Chomsky, 1969.

SECONDARY PREDICATORS

PREPOSITIONS

Prepositional phrases share many properties with relative clauses. The constituent to which they append serves as the antecedent which they modify. The preposition designates a relationship between the antecedent and an object. Although it is customary to think of predicators in a narrow sense, i.e. as verbs only, we shall expand the taxonomy of predicators to include the referential relationships denoted by prepositions. This will permit us to incorporate prepositional phrases into the theoretical framework of this study.[1] We will consider prepositional phrases to be predications, or, in other words, a special type of sentence (henceforth annotated SP). It is customary to refer to the object of a preposition. Acknowledging the significance of the proposals just made, we note that the referent which an SP modifies also functions as its subject (Figure 6.1).

Prepositional phrases modify all major constituent categories, even entire sentences. The rewrite rules which adjoin prepositions and their subjects must therefore show the subject as a variable: SP → X PP. An additional rule PP → P NP adjoins a preposition to an object. It is obvious that many things may be predicated of nouns, but what of the other categories? For them it is natural to specify time, place, manner, frequency, aspect, tense, etc.

ADJECTIVES AND ADVERBS

We shall include adjectives within the class of predicators as well. A similar reclassification of adverbs is in order, if it can be shown that they are an autonomous category. Many adverbs appear to be derivative, i.e. reduced prepositional phrases. Others are

---

[1] Our proposal in this chapter to enlarge the class of predicators to include prepositions (particles), adjectives, and adverbs is not an innovation. This point of view is certainly not foreign to symbolic logic (see Reichenbach, 1966) nor to current syntactic theory (see Langendoen, 1969). What is new, so far as we know, is the incorporation of clausal and phrasal modifiers into the overall inventory of syntactic structures under a single grammatical relationship (X/Y S).

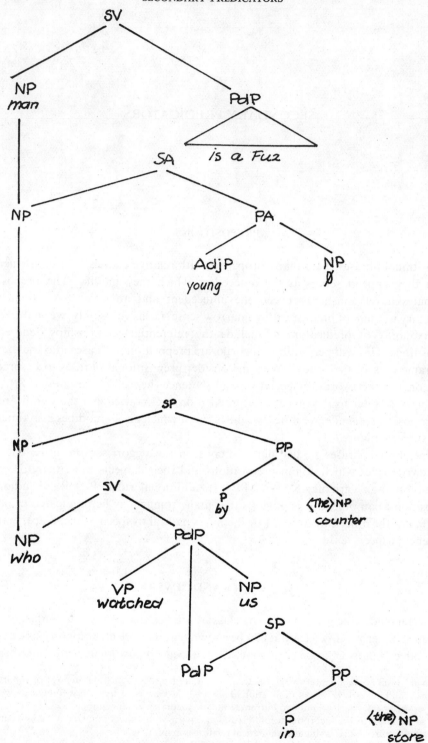

Fig. 6.1. Mixed sequential modifiers.

awkward to analyse in this fashion (such adverbs as *soon, often, seldom*). For the present we assume that adverbs not deriving from underlying PP's do not form an independent category, but are, with adjectives, manifestations of a more general category which we shall designate A. Predications having A as their predicative nuclei will be designated SA, which is expanded by the rules SA → X PA and PA[2] → AP NP. X will allow A modifiers of nouns, adjectives, adverbs, verbs, and perhaps prepositions (note compounds such as *onto, into*, etc.).

To avoid misunderstanding, it should be noted that we do not propose that prepositions and adjectives are verbs. Rather, we propose that verbs, adjectives/adverbs, and prepositions are predicators. They share a common property which permits them to function as the nucleus around which arguments may be organized to form predications. We assume tacitly that any modifying structure contains such a nucleus, being predicative of certain facts relative to an antecedent.

The variable formula X/Y S is adequate in its present form to subjoin both primary (with a V nucleus) and secondary predications (with A or P nuclei) if the symbol S is redefined as a variable ranging over the predicational categories SV (verbal nucleus), SA (adjectival or adverbial nucleus), and SP (prepositional nucleus). The structural representation of a sentence which contains all three types of modifiers is given in Figure 6.1.

Notice that it is now possible to subordinate adjectives and prepositional phrases to nouns independently of a relative clause containing a copula. If $r' \neq \emptyset$, subjoined SA predications will be restrictive: *Large delicious ripe red apples*... Conversely, if $r' = \emptyset$, the adjective will be nonrestrictive with the same properties as other such modifiers:[3] *The industrious Chinese*. Sequential SP predications may be subjoined in a similar fashion, or a mixture of the three, as is the case in the sentence represented in Figure 6.1.

Regardless of predicational category, the values of r and r' presupposed for the antecedent will determine whether the modifier is restricted or nonrestricted. We emphasize again that a decision to derive nonrestrictive relative clauses from conjoined sentences has ramifications for a host of other modifiers, many of which cannot be derived from conjuncts in any obvious way.

A NOTATIONAL ADJUSTMENT

At this point we wish to make an adjustment in the notation of subjunction rules. Until now we have written as the last element of subjunction rules the node dominating the entire subordinate structure. Henceforth we shall write instead the node of the subordinate structure which immediately dominates the point of intersection (see

[2] The need for an intermediate level node (PA) becomes clear when nominalized adjectives are considered. See Lytle, 1971, 162–165.

[3] See pp. 51–52.

Figure 6.2). This modification will enable us to differentiate by rule between P-markers which yield *who* (subject; NP/NP S); *whom* (direct object; NP/NP PdP), *to whom* (object of preposition; NP/NP PP), etc. Accordingly we revise the subjunction formula (X/Y S), replacing the S with D, a variable which is allowed to range over predicate level as well as predication level nodes (X/Y D).

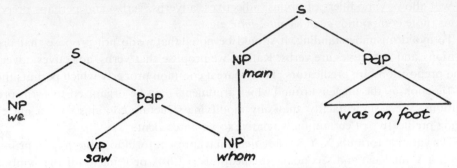

Fig. 6.2. A P-marker illustrating NP/NP PdP.

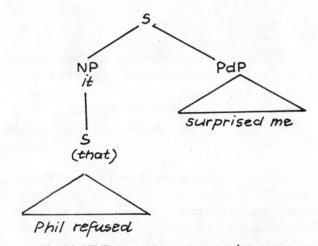

Fig. 6.3. NP/S represents a sentence used as a noun.

In those instances where the entire subordinate structure falls within the categorial brackets of the antecedent (Figure 6.3), the third node label of the rule will be suppressed. Thus, instead of writing NP/S S ("NP subjoin S of S"), where both S labels represent the same node, we will simply write NP/S. Suppression of the third node label in subjunction rules occurs for all configurations which we have referred to as abstract sentential constituents.[4]

The addition of new symbols to the inventory of categories in conjunction with the notational adjustments discussed above has the immediate effect of expanding the

[4] See chapter 5, p. 63.

number of possible rules in the system. While it is beyond the scope of this study to discuss each possibility separately, illustrative P-markers for many of them are given in Appendix II with a brief comment about each.

NODE LABELS

Whereas predication-level nodes (SV, SP, SA) are consistent in reflecting the category of their predicative nuclei, one predicate-level node is not (*PdP, PA, PP). For the sake of consistency, we shall henceforth dispense with PdP and write PV (predicate with a verbal nucleus) instead. So far as other labels are concerned, the use of NP, VP, AdjP, and AdvP for terminal nodes is problematical. However, since a discussion of the alternatives would lead us far afield, we shall reserve further comment on this matter for a subsequent writing.[5]

---

[5]   Provisionally, we may say that a noun phrase consists of a noun plus its modifiers, a verb phrase consists of a verb plus its modifiers, etc. The 'phrase' (P) part of categorial labels can be eliminated if this line of reasoning is pursued to its logical conclusion. In other words, NP, VP, AdjP, etc. can be replaced by N, V, Adj, etc. For further discussion, see Lytle, 1971, 142–144.

7

THE GENERAL STRUCTURE OF REFERENCE

Conceivably, there could be a language with no common nouns, so that every nominal referent would have its unique lexical symbol – a proper noun. The same would be true of other lexical categories as well. One suspects, however, that such a language would be a reflection of the environment in which it evolved – an environment based strictly on individuals, not on classes and individuals. In that unusual world two instances of a single type would not occur. Every animal would constitute a unique species. Every act, quality, quantity, characteristic or event would be completely unrelated to any other.

The reader has no doubt noticed that language in such a strange world would constitute a paradox. The act of speaking, each time it occurs, is a recurring phenomenon. Moreover, the structure of language itself is based on recursive structural types. The concept of simplicity through generality is based on this very notion. Language in such a world would not be the familiar phenomenon we know, but an individual occurrence, a single event, which, having taken place once, could never occur again. Moreover, at the single instance when it did occur, every lexical category, every structure, every word would be unique. There could never be another instance of it. And so on.

Such philosophizing is pointless, perhaps, except that it makes us more aware of the structure of our own environment as we perceive it and its reflection in human language. Although it is popular to question the legitimacy of our perception on philosophical grounds, there is little scientific justification for taking those arguments seriously. The concept of natural selection, for example, does not question the ability of living organisms to perceive environmental conditions. I doubt, for example, that you would find an animal putting on extra hair as a result of 'presupposed' climatic conditions, or any scientist using such adjectives in his description of evolutionary processes. If physical perception is reducible to the operation of physical laws as a result of the structure of sensory organs, 'meta-'physics need not enter the discussion at all. In other words, if the form of human perception is physically imposed, we may accept it as correct, much as we accept without question the perceptive analysis of temperature given by a thermometer. This is not to say that perceptive differences of the same environment do not occur. They do, of course, but in matters of detail for the most part, which are insignificant considering the overall context of perceptual uniformity. It is convenient for the descriptive linguist to assume that linguistic structure is not an arbitrary phenomenon, differing from language to language and person to person, but a natural selection dependent upon the structure of our surroundings. This makes language a natural rather than a supernatural phenomenon, bringing it within reach of scientific investigation and description.

We perceive a world organized in terms of classes and sub-classes. Individuals generally occur as specializations of types, as reflected by non-restrictivization. In order to intercommunicate, it must be that we refer to the phenomena and events of our experience within the framework of our common perception. This in turn suggests that the general structure of linguistic reference is a reflection of perceptual structure. Otherwise, vicarious perception via the intermediary of language would not be possible.

Assuming that our perception is in terms of sets and members of sets, language must provide a means for identifying intended referents uniquely. This procedure as it now emerges is as follows: (1) The non-unique properties of the referent are established by naming it, i.e. by associating with it a word which designates a particular class of referents. (2) Identifying properties of the referent are then given by modification, the syntactic operation of subjunction providing the formal vehicle for this portion of the referential act. The generality of the recursive formula X/Y D provides for modifiers on all major lexical categories. Actually, this is to be expected, since lexical categories other than nouns may also be common. If the subjunction could not apply to them, referential specialization (focus) could not be achieved. An utterance, then, may be viewed as a structured sequence of referent specifications.

Interestingly, application of the subordinator extends beyond lexical categories to syntactic categories, so that it is possible to construct modifiers for complex constituents. Sentence level modifiers of the various possible sorts are in this category. We may conclude, then, that sememes are not restricted as to internal scope – they may be complex as well as simple.

The values r and r' have been shown to exist for constituents of diverse categories and complexity. This indicates that we conceptualize complex as well as simple entities within the same framework. In short, sememes are evaluated as unique or non-unique, regardless of internal complexity. This property of referential structure appears not to be language dependent, but a universal imposed upon all languages by the form of human perception.

The traditional analysis of sentence structures in terms of constituents and their modifiers *cannot* be dismissed as a manifestation of linguistic naïveté. That analysis is intuitively correct. The formula X/Y D expresses the relationship of antecedent to modifier. The application or non-application of subjunction, as we conceive of it, has semantic significance, since it underlies referential specialization. To move constituents about will of necessity alter modificational relationships to some degree. The position that transformations may alter structure but not meaning is difficult to defend in this context. In general, it must be concluded that the concept of transformation is incompatible with the concept of modification. This need not be troublesome, however. The need for transformational operations seems to diminish as significant linguistic generalities are discovered.

8

EVALUATION AND APPLICATION

EVALUATION

At this juncture it seems appropriate to attempt an evaluation of the total picture, relating what we have sought to accomplish with what has been achieved in the past.

We note first of all that many linguists and language specialists have been frustrated by transformational-generative grammar. They were earnestly searching for and expecting developments in linguistic theory which would have immediate practical application. These expectations were in many instances not realized. Advances in pedagogical techniques deriving from transformational grammar are not impressive. In fact, the technique receiving most attention in recent years, the oral-aural method, smacks of behaviorism, the antithesis of what transformationalists postulate as the underlying psychology of language acquisition. As a tool for such technical tasks as mechanical translation, transformational grammar has not provided definitive solutions, although it has provided the basis for a great deal of interesting research. Theory-wise, transformational grammar is now troubled by problems of the sort discussed in Chapter 2. As we have seen, the transformational school is criticized by McCawley and others[1] who feel that the transformational approach has neglected semantics. We believe that this is a just criticism.

On the positive side, transformational-generative grammar has succeeded in demonstrating the need for having a well-defined linguistic theory to approach the descriptive analysis of language. It has demonstrated the need for a rigorous description of linguistic structures rather than a loose verbal one. It has awakened the interest of specialists in many related fields and stimulated inter-disciplinary communication. It has drawn attention to the strategic importance of linguistic science as the fulcrum of many disciplines.

It is difficult to say how the theoretical modifications suggested in this study may affect the overall picture. The genenerality of subjunction as herein formalized describes and organizes a mass of linguistic data which otherwise seemed unrelated.

[1]   Chafe, 1970.

The linguist cannot help being enthusiastic when a linguistic generality appears to have been captured. A wider range of syntactic structures is now directly generable (i.e. by P-rules), thus eliminating so far as these are concerned the need for transformational manipulation.

Although the authors of transformational theory have taken pains to point out their dependence upon and continuation of the linguistic past, the differences are somehow more prominent than the similarities. A synthesis and reconciliation of generative grammar with certain tenets of traditional grammar seems to derive from the approach we propose. This, perhaps, may constitute the most significant contribution of the study. Formalization of the modificational relationship along generative lines while maintaining the traditional distinction between conjunction and subordination makes the link with the past more credible.

For some time efforts have been directed toward constraining the virtually unlimited power (and hence variety) of transformations.[2] One might anticipate that legitimate constraints would have the effect of identifying specific types of rules, thus limiting the scope of possible rules to an inventory of specialized grammatical operations. Such a result would be welcome, of course, since the construction of grammars would then become something more than a hit and miss exercise, the number of possible rules for a given language being severely restricted. In fact, the notion of a discovery procedure for grammars could then be seriously reconsidered.[3]

Our proposals may be construed as an attempt to constrain transformations by abstracting away functions which seem more appropriately assigned to other rule components. Adjunction, conjunction, and subjunction are grammatical operations defining junction between constituents, and delineate a specific rule component in the grammar (junction rules). L-rules construct lexical strings corresponding to Level II representations, i.e. they map sememes into lexemes. These rules perform an entirely different function than those which define junction. It is these rules which must now explicate the morphology of particular languages. Phonological rules of the form discussed in the literature presumably constitute another distinct component of rules in the grammar.

It is not really paradoxical, perhaps, that there is no specific set of rules remaining which can be called the 'transformational component'. Rules of various sorts originally thrown together under one name are subsumed under more descriptive labels according to their specialized functions in the grammar. The one possible rule candidate for a transformational component would be the kind of rule that actually alters structure, subordinating constituents which were originally conjoined, and so forth. We have excluded this type of operation on theoretical grounds, believing it to be incompatible with the general structure of reference as we have presented it. Actually, we see no need for structure-changing rules so far as tree-generation is concerned. It

[2]   Ross, 1967. See also Emonds, 1969; Peters, 1969; Postal, 1969; and Chomsky, 1969.
[3]   Peters, 1969.

appears that any well-formed structure is directly generable if the base rules are formalized correctly. It remains to be seen, of course, whether specific semantic arguments for transformation can be answered in all cases.[4]

As to the prospects for outlining a discovery procedure for grammars on the basis of results deriving from this study, the inventory of rules subsumed under X/Y D has promise. The specializations of the formula (summarized in Appendix II) appear not to be English-bound, but represent structures which occur in human languages generally. It is probably a safe assumption that subordinate structures which can be constructed in English are possible in most other languages. Assuming this to be the case, the working grammarian simply proceeds to identify the predicted range of subjunctions in the language being described, constructing L-rules to account for the particular morphological system utilized in their lexical realization. A similar approach is possible for anticipating what languages will have in the way of adjoined or conjoined structures.

The theory suggests an analytical approach to data as well. One will first wish to determine the nature of junction between constituents, i.e. whether a particular lexical constituent is an adjunct, conjunct, or subjunct of adjacent constituents. Having decided, for example, that a particular constituent is subordinated, one must next seek out evidence to indicate whether subjunction is homogeneous or heterogeneous, and in either case whether the antecedent is AdvP, NP, VP, SV, or a node of some other category.

APPLICATION

The following applications of the theory suggest themselves:

Syntactic Analysis

Continued descriptive analysis of linguistic structures along the same lines is in order. There are obviously many structures yet to be accounted for. The goal would be to identify and provide for the direct generation of all syntactic structures. The theory will, of course, undergo modification and elaboration as this task proceeds.

Pedagogy

The organization of language teaching materials around the inventory of syntactic structures provided by the theory and in harmony with the theory of linguistic reference as we have presented it may be fruitful. The inherent linguistic capacity defended by Chomsky and his associates appears to be authentic, corresponding to the linguistic activity postulated for Level II. These aspects of language acquisition seem to be instinctive, i.e. unconditioned. Assuming that linguistic structure at this level is uni-

---

[4] See Lytle, 1971 for further discussion.

versal, acquiring a second language involves learning at other levels, namely Levels III and IV (lexicalization and pronunciation respectively). It is indisputable that these levels incorporate a significant noninstinctive element, which means that acquisition of the vocabulary and morphophonemics of the target language will entail conditioning. Thus, in a sense, advocates of both theories of learning appear to be correct, and certain ingredients of the several pedagogical approaches are also correct. Specifically, the idea that universal (intuitive) aspects of grammar need not be disproportionately dwelt upon seems justified. Similarly, words and expressions (or morphophonemic patterns) not amenable to intuitive acquisition will have to be explained (related to the student's native language) and conditioned by drills. The identification of language-specific lexical rules may provide a natural format for preparing these materials.

More importance should be attributed to rapid acquisition of vocabulary, so that the student has the lexical stock necessary to make reference to objects in the target language. Stronger incentives should be devised to stimulate lexical learning in correlation with frequent opportunities to use newly learned lexicon.

With respect to the organization of pedagogical grammars, the theory provides an extensive inventory of possible sentence and phrase structures which might occur in any human language. This inventory can serve as an objective basis for providing a comprehensive but nonredundant content for grammars, progressing from the most trivial to the most complex structures.

The nature of meaning as we have presented it suggests that language acquisition may be stimulated by creating situations which correspond to the semantic content of language materials, so that communication within the target language is both natural and necessary. The student deserves to learn language in such a way that the referential act is not artificial but spontaneous.

Activities which entail intensive conditioning could be scheduled out of class, and would incorporate the best that programmed learning and audio-visual presentation techniques have to offer. The creative use of language (this would be emphasized from the outset) would take place in a classroom or other more appropriate environment under the supervision of an instructor.

The development of materials for the presentation of descriptive grammar in primary and secondary schools may prove beneficial. Composition and speech activities could be centered around a conscious awareness of syntactic operations and the structure of reference. Drills in the manipulation of syntactic structures might possibly be developed to promote speech sophistication at an early age.

Speech Therapy

The theory may possibly have fruitful application in speech therapy. A diagnostic test could be devised to evaluate the range and effectiveness of sentence structuring in persons whose speech is abnormal. Corrective exercises could perhaps be organized to fill in structural gaps or induce patterns not being manipulated effectively. The goal would be to treat syntactic impediments as effectively as articulatory impediments.

Psycho-linguistic S

There is a need to test the theory against observed psychological processes of perception and conceptualization.

Automatic Translation

It can be reported at this time that a pilot application of the theory to machine translation[5] has yielded encouraging results. The concept of structural translation is actually feasible if structures are dealt with directly rather than transformationally. Linguists should commit themselves to achieving an accurate automatic translation of oral language before the turn of this century, and financial sources should support that effort.

Literary Analysis

The theory is applicable to literary criticism as an extension of formalism. The search for structural bases of literary style will become increasingly more successful as our knowledge of linguistic structures and operations improves. A computer programmed for translation could provide structural statistics for a given text on short notice. This would greatly expedite and facilitate formal analyses of literary works.

Communication

The intermediate Level II representation constructed by a translation program could be telemetrically transmitted and resynthesized at distant locations as desired. As a code the transmission would be secure. As a telemetric signal it would transmit when direct oral transmission would fail. Resynthesis of the transmission would be language independent, i.e. the transmission would be reconstituted in Russian, French, Spanish, etc., depending upon what language-specific interpretive grammar is employed by the receiving computer. Such a capability would have many applications, of course, remote space communication being one of them.

Comparative Linguistics

A comparative survey of a wide range of non-Indo-European languages is needed to test the assumption that the modificational patterns predicted by the theory are universal.

---

[5]   Gibb, 1970. Translation research at Brigham Young University (Provo, Utah) is currently testing the theory in its application to English, Russian, Spanish, Portuguese, French, German and Japanese.

Phonology

A priority application for the results of this study would appear to be the use of phrase structures generated by a 'junction' grammar as the basis for phonological analysis. The output of the grammar corresponds closely to natural phrasing. The use of three types of junction (rather than the usual two) seems to provide phrase structure capable of supporting phonological interpretation without supplementary adjustments.[6]

[6]   See p. 31, this study.

LEXICAL RULES

Lexical rules (L-rules) construct lexical strings corresponding to Level II representations for a particular language. Although lexical rules vary from language to language, there are presumably universals which specify the form of such rules and the manner in which they may apply. Context sensitivity is apparently a universal formal property of lexical rules. We illustrate below various forms of lexical rules. It will be noted that each rule applies in a given environment.

Since we consider the structural disposition of constituents to be an essential part of their meaning, L-rules perform an interpretive function only. They reflect rather than alter Level II representations. L-rules perform the following specialized operations: (1) They match constituent indices with the lexemes corresponding to them; (2) they insert affixes; (3) they govern the order in which constituents appear in the surface structure; (4) they exempt constituents from lexicalization in given environments. In general, L-rules determine the morphology of a particular language. In this sense, the L-rules constitute a morphological component in the grammar. Let us consider illustrative rules of English for each of the functions we have identified.

MATCHING

Words such as *tree* and *water* correspond to specific referents at Level II. Since it is not possible to use concepts to represent themselves, neutral indices are used in their place. The expression

$$\text{Sememe} \rightarrow \text{Lexeme} \ / \ [\text{------}]$$

shows the format for L-rules which match Level II constituents with Level III constituents. Specific rules for *tree* and *water* are:

$$E \rightarrow tree \quad / \ [\text{------}] \\ .0001$$

$$E \rightarrow water \quad / \ [\text{------}] \\ .0002$$

The arrow represents the matching operation. The diagonal means 'in the environ-ment'. The horizontal line ([————]) identifies the sememe undergoing lexicalization. The rules read in the following manner: A sememe (E) is lexicalized as *tree* if it is the index .0001. In this instance, .0001 and .0002 are purely arbitrary. Obviously, the assignment of numerical indices to large numbers of vocabulary items requires a systematic code.

AFFIXES

The placement of affixes requires a lexical as well as a referential environment, since they may appear as suffixes, prefixes, or infixes. In other words, the rules must not only specify what E is realized on the affix, but where that affix must occur in relation to a particular stem. This can be accomplished by adding a second environment (a lexical environment) to the rule:

$$E \rightarrow \text{affix} / [\text{———}] \quad : \quad \begin{cases} [\text{stem}]\text{———} & (1) \\ \text{———}[\text{stem}] & (2) \\ [[\ ]\text{———}[\ ]] & (3) \end{cases}$$

The environment specified to the right of the colon is strictly lexical. (1) places a suffix; (2) places a prefix; and (3) places an infix. The lexical environment, of course, can be as complicated or as simple as the occasion requires. The rule which places [+ness] on nominalized adjectives would assume the following form:

$$E \rightarrow +ness / \quad \overline{\text{NP}} \quad : \quad [_1\text{Adj}] \ \text{———}$$

CONCORD AND AGREEMENT

Rather than copying features from nouns, for example, onto constituents found in morphological concord with them, lexical rules simply insert morphemes into fixed positions in the lexical string when given features are present in the governing noun. Thus, the suffix +s on the verb in *John speaks* is a marker which occurs on the verb if the subject is 3rd person singular.

$$E \rightarrow +s / \text{NP} \quad \left\langle \begin{array}{c} \text{———} \\ \text{3rd person} \\ \text{singular} \end{array} \right\rangle \quad \begin{bmatrix} \text{PV} \\ [\text{Vi}] \ldots \end{bmatrix} \quad : \quad \begin{array}{c} [\text{stem}]\text{———} \\ \text{Vi} \\ <\text{present}> \end{array}$$

is a complex symbol of features presupposed by the speaker about the subject.

ORDERING

We consider word order to be governed by language-specific conventions. Ordering rules do not alter the order of Level II constituents, but govern the order in which lexical interpretation is to proceed. The dominant order in English is subject-verb-object (SVO). There are variations, however. Moreover, auxiliary inversion is used to mark interrogative sentences; adverbials are optionally preposed, and so forth. To explain such facts about word order, we posit lexical ordering (LO) rules. For example, the following rule places interrogative *did*:

$$(1)\ E \rightarrow did\ /\ \begin{bmatrix} \quad \end{bmatrix}\ \left\langle \begin{array}{c} \underline{\quad\quad} \\ past \\ \langle interr \rangle_1 \end{array} \right\rangle \quad : \quad \begin{cases} \langle -\ [N] \ldots [V] \rangle_1 & (1) \\ [N] \ldots - [V] & (2) \end{cases}$$

Numbered angles ($\langle\ \rangle_1$) indicate a systematic co-occurrence constraint between discontinuous constituents. The rule stipulates that *did* marks $\begin{array}{c} past \\ interr \end{array}$ in lexical environment (1), or *(past)* in environment (2). The environments are disjunctive.[1]

The L-rules given below impose a specific order upon the lexicalization of major constituents:

$$L\ (S) \rightarrow \underset{1}{NP} \quad \underset{2}{PV}$$

$$L\ (PV) \rightarrow \underset{1}{VP} \quad \begin{Bmatrix} NP \\ AdjP \\ 2 \end{Bmatrix}$$

These rules are to be read: The lexicalization of S and PV, respectively, proceeds in the order indicated.[2]

---

[1] The insertion rule for *did* is given here *ad hoc*. Obviously, other auxiliaries are also preposed in the presence of an interrogative feature in English.

[2] Ordering operations may also be construed as language specific constraints imposed upon the application of P-rules. The details of this approach are discussed in Lytle, forthcoming.

HIATUS

The last type of rule we propose is an instruction to omit the lexicalization of given constituents. The effect of such rules is that lexical absence is sufficient to indicate presence at Level II. Thus, the absence of a subject in the sentence *Leave immediately* suffices to indicate the presence of imperative *you* in the Level II representation.

$$E \rightarrow \emptyset \;/\; [\ldots] $$
$$\text{NP} \qquad \left\langle \begin{array}{c} \text{2nd person} \\ \text{imperative} \end{array} \right\rangle$$

E is lexically null (not deleted) in the environment indicated.

Obviously, the lexical component of grammars will be as intricate and complex as the morphological systems they attempt to describe. For this reason, we believe it preferable to relegate such language-specific operations to the interpretive grammars of particular languages.

Considerable attention is presently being given to so-called output conditions or filter rules which appear necessary to account for the non-occurrence or awkwardness of certain sentences which seem perfectly well-formed in their deep structure. Thus, in a sentence such as *someone came, didn't*———? there is hesitation as to which pronoun should occur in the blank. *He* and *she* have specific gender; *someone* does not. *Someone* is singular; *they* is plural.

The problem in this instance is clearly a feature of English morphology. The L-rules which insert *he*, *she*, and *they* are constrained by an environment specified in terms of gender and number in such a way that said environment is not satisfied by the constituent '———?' in the tag question being considered. There is no English pronoun which is entirely appropriate in this context.

It seems obvious that constraints of this sort should find their expression in rules which govern the morphology of English, rather than in rules which impose Level II constraints. Within the theoretical framework we have elaborated, L-rules (which constitute the interpretive grammar of English) provide a format for the explication of linguistic phenomena such as this.

AN INVENTORY OF SUBJUNCTION RULES IN ENGLISH

We give below a list of subjunction rules for which examples are found in English. Each rule is accompanied by:

(a) A brief statement suggesting how strings corresponding to the rule may be recognized;
(b) Data from English exemplifying the rule; and
(c) A P-marker illustrating the example.

1. NP/NP SV

(a) A relative clause with a nominal antecedent. The relative pronoun functions as the subject of the subordinate clause.
(b) Students who study succeed.
(c)

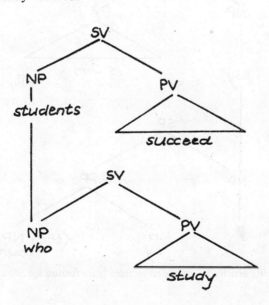

2. NP/NP PV

(a) A relative clause with a nominal antecedent. The relative pronoun, sometimes suppressed, functions as the direct object of the subordinate clause.

(b) The item (that) he purchased was expensive.

(c)

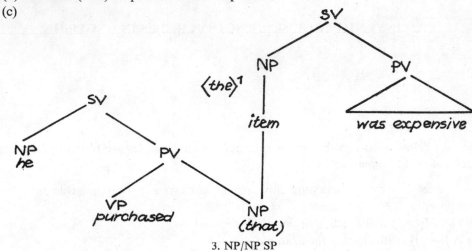

3. NP/NP SP

(a) A prepositional phrase modifying a nominal antecedent. The antecedent sememe is the subject of the preposition.

(b) The boy by the counter is Jim.

(c)

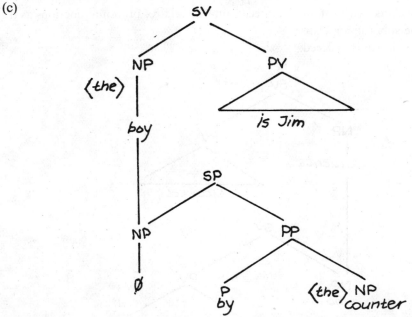

---

[1] Definite and indefinite articles are assumed to stem from feature specifications on NP, not from separate nodes.

4. NP/NP PP

(a) A prepositional phrase, part of a subordinate clause, has a nominal antecedent in the main clause. The antecedent sememe is the object (rather than the subject) of the preposition. Dangling prepositions are a lexical option provided by English for these constructions.

(b) The friend I wrote to (to whom I wrote) lives in England.

(c)

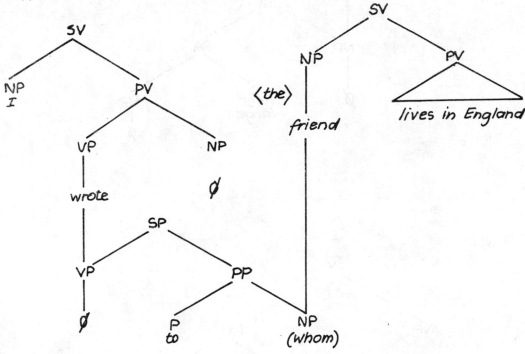

5. NP/NP SA

(a) A nominal sememe is modified by an adjective construction. If the adjective sememe is that of possession, it will be transitive, i.e. it will have a nominal adjoined to it in the object position (compare *John's/of John; the boy's/of the boy;* etc.). If the nominal adjunct of the possessive also has modifiers, the 'floating' *'s* of English results (see [b] (3) below).

(b) (1) A large dog chased me.

    (2) Your slip is showing.

    (3) The man who came to dinner's coat was soiled. (cf. The coat of the man who came to dinner.)

(c) (1)

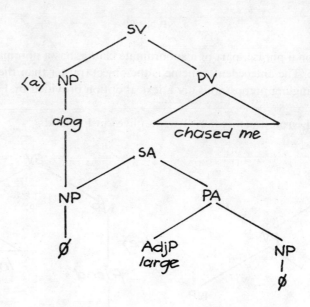

(c) (2)

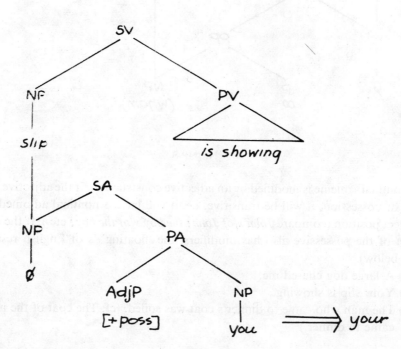

(c) (3)

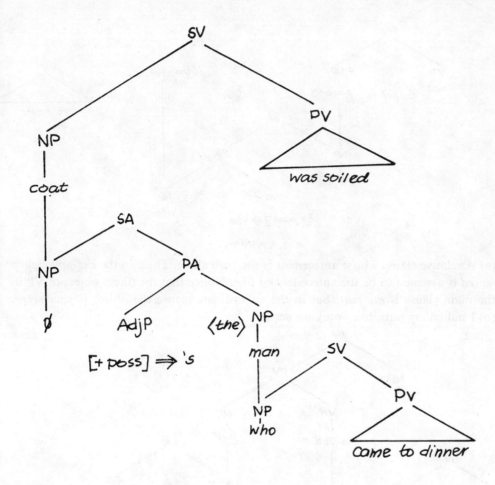

6. NP/NP PA

(a) This is the rule which yields 'possessive' relative clauses, i.e. where the relative pronoun is *whose*. If the possessive sememe is recategorized as a preposition, then the rule would be NP/NP PP (see rule 4), and *of whom* would result.
(b) The girl whose parents (the parents of whom) you met left home.

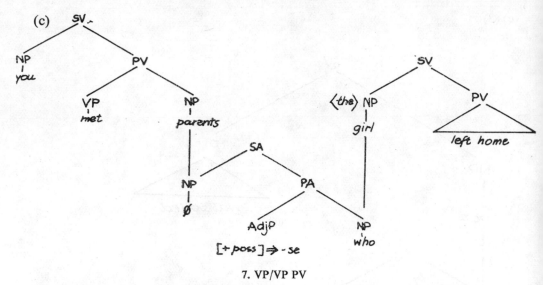

7. VP/VP PV

(a) A relative clause whose antecedent is the verb alone. Thus, in the example below *miffed* is assumed to be the antecedent of *like*. Notice that the direct object of VP in the main clause is *my putt*, but in the subordinate clause the object is *your serve*.

(b) I miffed my putt, like you your serve.

(c)

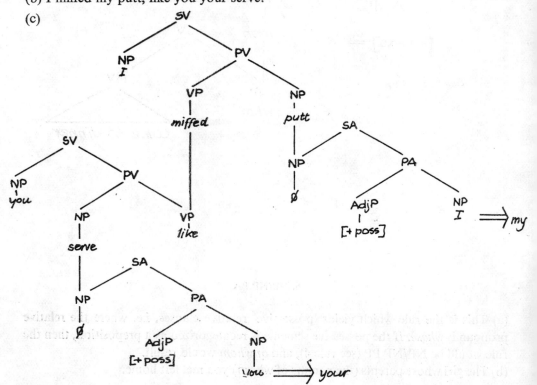

8. VP/VP SP

(a) A prepositional phrase modifying a verbal sememe (exclusive of any direct object). If the prepositional sememe is dative, it is often suppressed (lexical hiatus), and its object is then referred to as the indirect object of the verb. Prepositional modifiers of this type generally convey the idea of motion, direction, or destination, as opposed to static location, manner, time, or accompaniment (for modifiers which convey these latter notions, see rule 16 below). In English, when the preposition is not suppressed, the modifier is discontinuous with the verb.

(b) Fred sent Susie a gift (*sent* a gift to *Susie*).

(c)

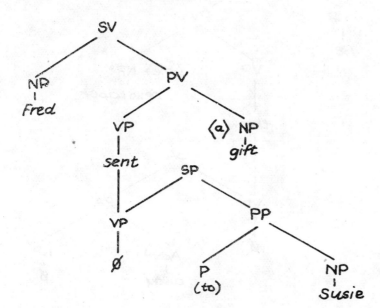

9. VP/VP SA

(a) The modifiers yielded by this rule are often referred to as verbal particles. They are adverbial sememes which specify the verb for aspect, motion, direction, etc. They are often discontinuous with the verb.

(b) He *threw* the newspaper *away*.

(c)

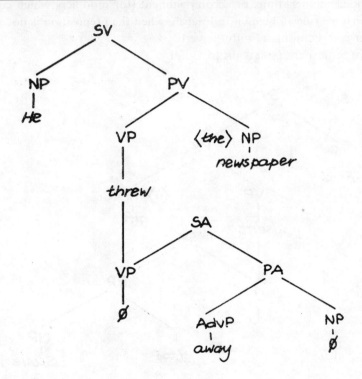

10. AdjP/AdjP PA

(a) This rule corresponds to modifiers linked by *like* or *as* to an adjective in the super-ordinate structure. The adjectival sememe is attributed simultaneously to distinct nominals in both independent and dependent structures. The rule is used to compare or contrast attributes of nominal sememes, or to identify unspecified attributes of one nominal by relating it to another whose attributes are known.

(b) People like (such as) you need help.

(c)

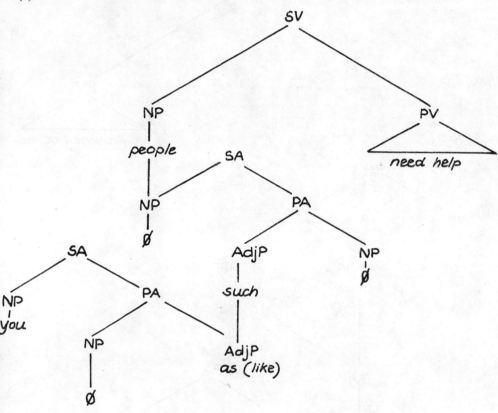

11. AdjP/AdjP SA

(a) An adverbial particle modifying an adjective.

(b) The unhappy man frowned at me.

(c)

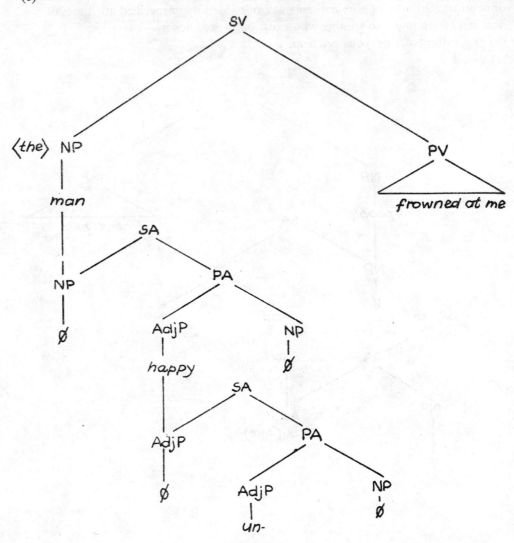

12. AdjP/AdjP SP

(a) This rule corresponds to prepositional modifiers which express the directionality of certain emotional states. They are to be contrasted with other prepositional modifiers which express degree, time, place, etc. (see rule 19).

(b) Persons happy with the results should so indicate.

(c)

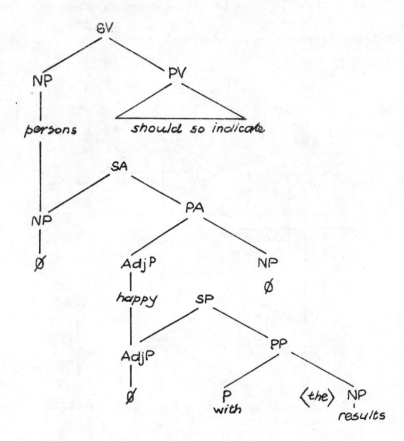

13. AdvP/AdvP PA

(a) This rule yields modifiers linked by *like* or *as* to an adverb in the superordinate structure (compare rule 10) in such a way that the adverbial sememe is attributed simultaneously to distinct predicates in both the dependent and independent clauses. The rule is used to compare or contrast attributes of predicates, or to identify unspecified attributes of one predicate by relating it to another whose attributes are known.

(b) You will reap like you sow (as ye sow, so shall ye reap).

(c)

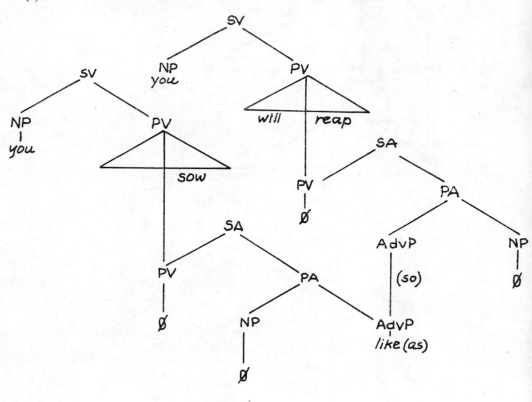

14. AdvP/AdvP SA

(a) This rule yields modifiers like those associated with rule 11, except that in this case the antecedent sememe must be adverbial rather than adjectival.

(b) The hand moves counter-clockwise.

(c)

15. P/P SA

(a) This rule may correspond to the compound prepositions which abound in English.
(b) A man without hope has a bleak future.
(c)

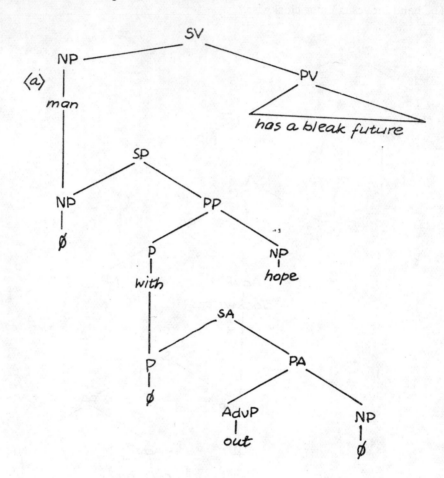

16. PV/PV SP

(a) Prepositional modifiers of predicates expressing time, place, manner, reason, etc. are the result of this rule.

(b) John smashed the window with a pipe.

(c)

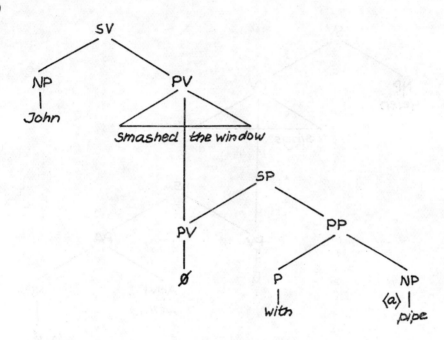

17. PV/PV SA

(a) These modifiers are like those yielded by rule 16, except that they are adverbial rather than prepositional.

(b) Helen sings well.

(c)

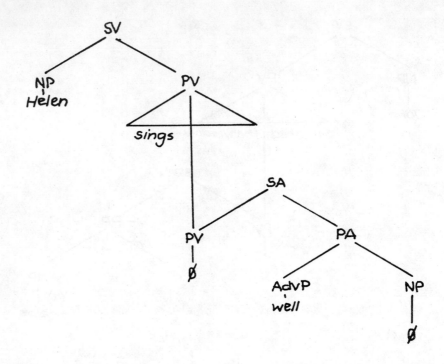

18. PV/PV SV

(a) The clausal modifiers yielded by this rule are always nonrestrictive. This is because they have complete predicates (unique entities) as antecedents. It should be noted that the omission of the comma (pause) would result in a string corresponding to the intersection of clauses on a manner adverbial (see rule 13), but not to PV/PV SV.

(b) Like you, I condemn violence.

(c)

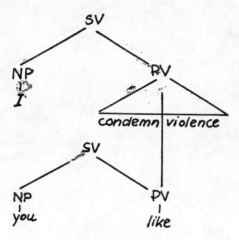

19. PA/PA SP

(a) Prepositional modifiers of adjective/adverb constructions conveying notions of degree, time, place, etc.

(b) Anyone tired without cause should see a doctor.

(c)

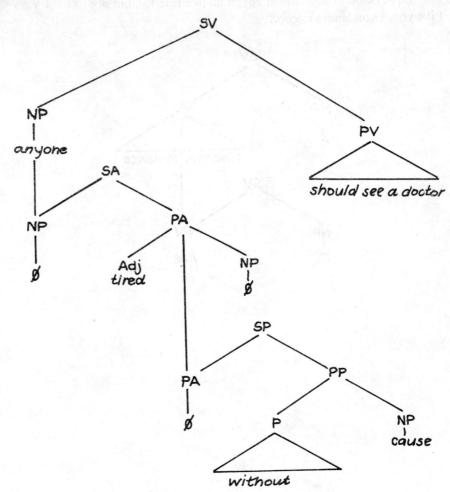

20. PA/PA SA

(a) These modifiers are like those yielded by rule 19, except that they are adverbial rather than prepositional.

(b) We saw a very bad accident.

(c)

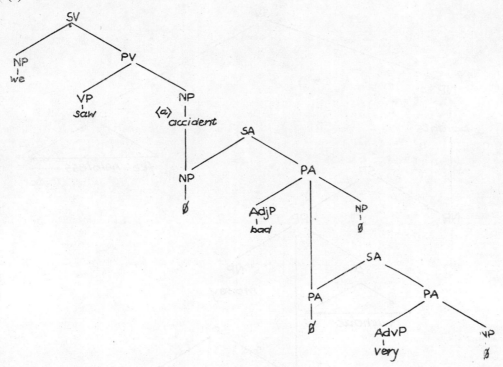

21. PP/PP SP

(a) This rule provides for modifiers of prepositional predicates. Such modifiers express degree, time, place, etc., like other PX level modifiers.
(b) Parents without money on Christmas feel helpless.
(c)

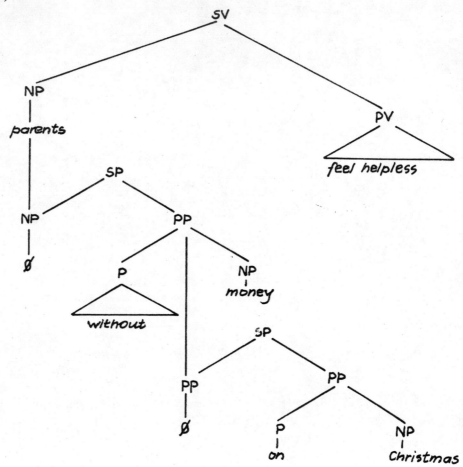

22. PP/PP SA

(a) This rule yields modifiers akın to those of rule 21, except that those corresponding to PP/PP SA are adverbial rather than prepositional.

(b) Dad put a bucket exactly under the leak.

(c)

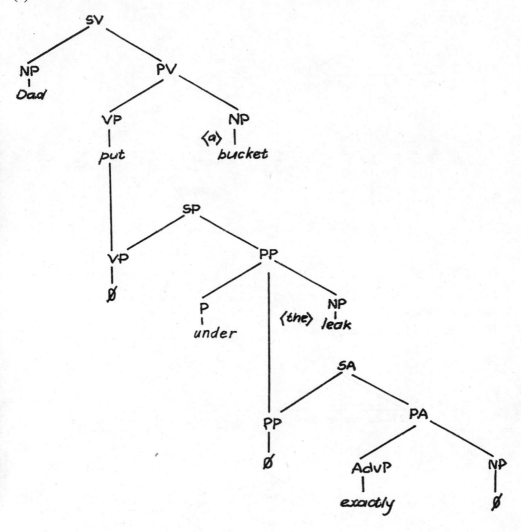

3. SV/SV SA

(a) Sentence adverbs correspond to this rule. Such modifiers generally express the attitude of the speaker about the content of the sentence, either from a logical or an emotional point of view (*unfortunately*, *surely*, *probably*, etc.).

(b) Actually, no one knew about it.

(c)

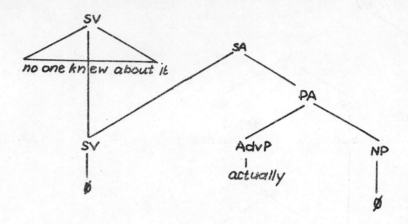

24. SV/SV SP

(a) This rule accounts for prepositional modifiers of sentences, which express notions similar to those identified for rule 23.

(b) In fact, I'll be there early.

(c)

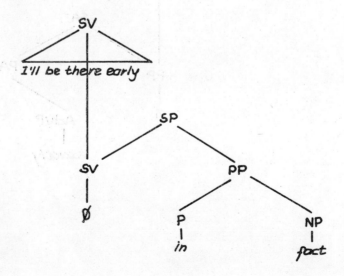

25. SP/SP SA

(a) Modifiers similar to those of rule 23, except that they qualify SP predications.

(b) A student purportedly on drugs murdered his roommate.

(c)

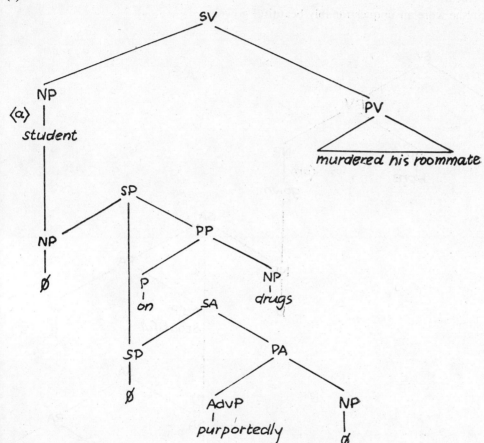

26. SA/SA SA

(a) This rule accounts for modifiers of adjectival/adverbial predications (compare rule 25). These, like other SX level modifiers, indicate how the speaker feels about the predication.

(b) She wore an unquestionably beautiful gown.

(c)

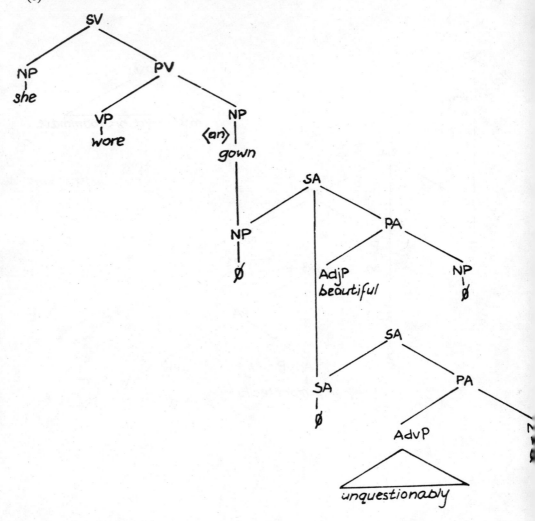

27. SA/SA SP

(a) These modifiers are like those yielded by rule 26, except that they are prepositional rather than adverbial. They have the same semantic properties as other SX level modifiers.

(b) A person very intelligent in my opinion was selected for the assignment.

(c)

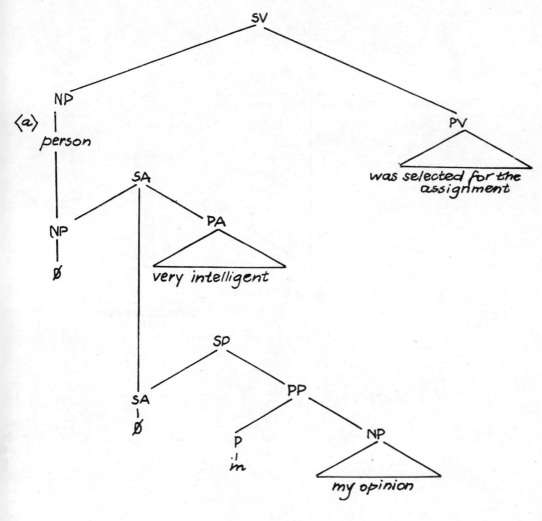

28. SV/NP SV

(a) This rule is for sentence relatives in which the main clause functions as the subject nominal of the dependent clause. If the rank of the clauses were reversed, an abstract sentential subject would result (NP/SV).

(b) The patient's condition has improved, which is encouraging (Inversion: It is encouraging that the patient's condition has improved).

(c)

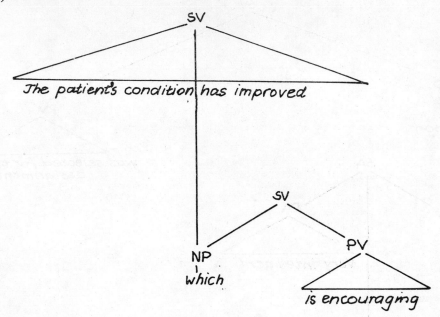

29. SV/NP PV

(a) If the relative pronoun of a sentence relative is the direct object of a verb, this rule has applied. Inversion of the clauses would yield an abstract sentential object.

(b) Bill always helps out, which I appreciate (Inversion: I appreciate it that Bill always helps out).

(c)

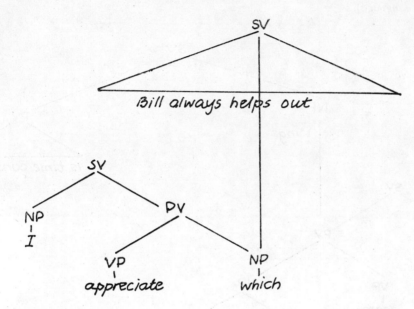

30. NP/PV SV

(a) This rule calls for a clausal predicate to function as a noun phrase. Nominalizations of this type occur either as gerundive forms in *-ing* or as infinitives marked by *to*. *It* is often used as a discontinuous antecedent for the infinitive forms.

(b) Learning a foreign language is time consuming (*It* is time consuming *to learn a foreign language*).

(c)

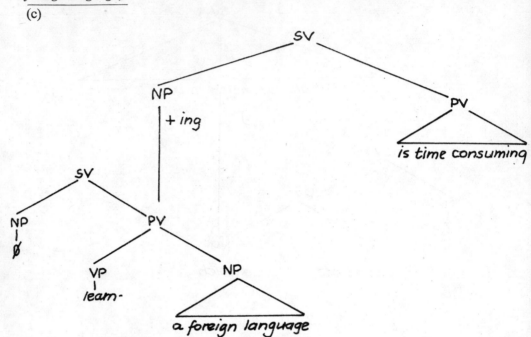

31. PV/NP SV

(a) This rule yields structures in which the antecedent of the relative pronoun is not a sentence but a predicate phrase. Since the third node label of the rule is SV, the relative pronoun will function as the subject of the dependent clause.

(b) Phil mastered the violin, which was a very difficult process.

(c)

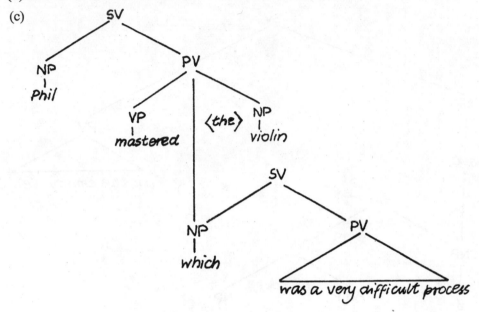

32. NP/VP PV

(a) The results of this rule are the 'action' nominals of English. Prepositions (*by* and *of*) often mark logical subjects and objects of the nominalized verb.

(b) The rejection of the proposal by the board disappointed us.

(c)

33. AdjP/SV

(a) The application of this rule is signaled by *such that* in English. *Such* marks the category (AdjP) of the antecedent, and *that* introduces the subordinate clause.
(b) A set such that it has no elements is the empty set.
(c)

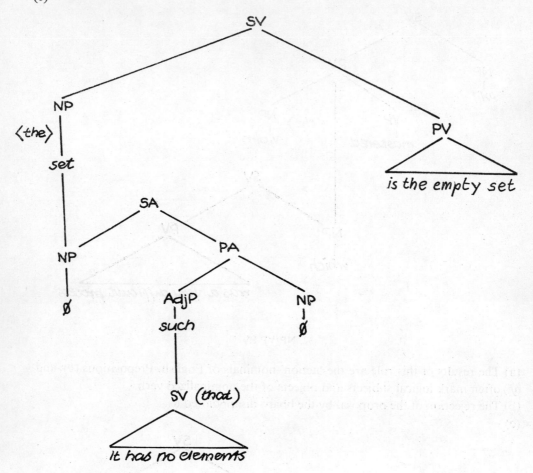

34. AdjP/PV SV

(a) Verbal adjectives commonly referred to as active and passive participles are produced by this rule. Since the suffixes marking these forms are used in other contexts also, one cannot attribute forms to AdjP/PV SV on the basis of suffixation alone. A legitimate passive is compatible with an agentive modifier marked by the preposition *by*. A legitimate active participle will be modifying a noun and can be paraphrased as a relative clause.

(b) (1) The money received by Ted was counterfeit.

(2) The lady washing dishes is Mrs. Jones.

(c) (1)

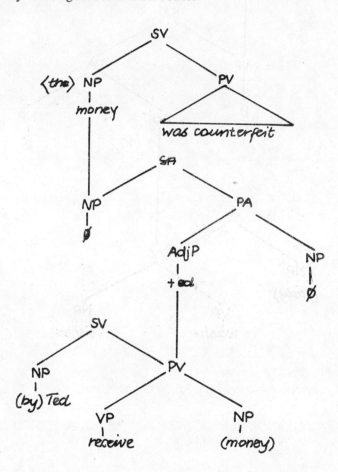

(c) (2)

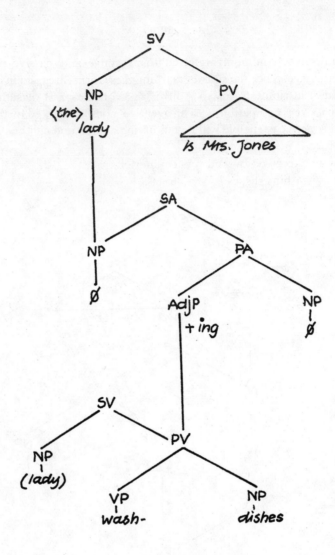

35. AdjP/VP PV

(a) Deverbal adjectives suffixed by *-ive* seem to satisfy the specifications of this rule. The logical subject of the internal VP will be the same as that of the AdjP to which it is subjoined. Logical objects, when they occur, are marked by the preposition *of*.

(b) We discovered clues indicative of foul play.

(c)

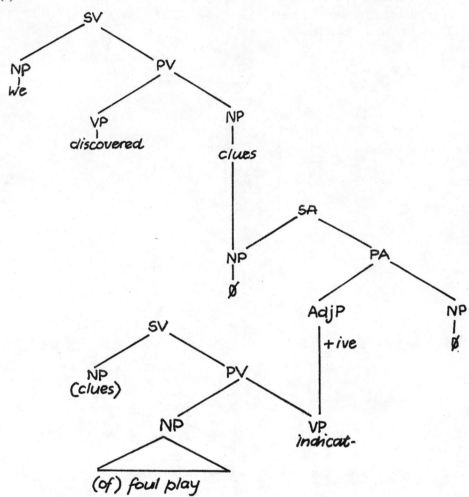

36. AdvP/SV

(a) Clauses introduced by *so that* are yielded by this rule. Other clauses linked to the main clause by *because*, *(as) if*, and *when* (if the clause is a complement rather than a relative clause) also correspond to this rule. In general, any adverbial complement seems to be the result of AdvP/SV.

(b) (1) We will leave when we have finished.

   (2) It rained, if the ground is wet.

   (3) She left home because she was bored.

(c) (1)

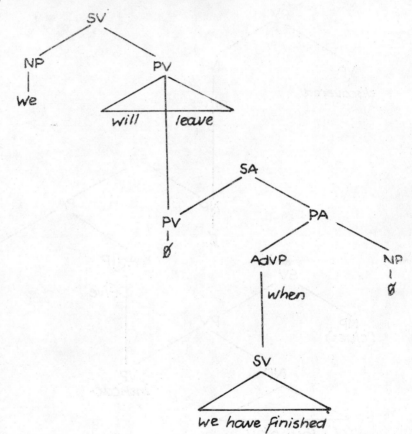

(c) (2)

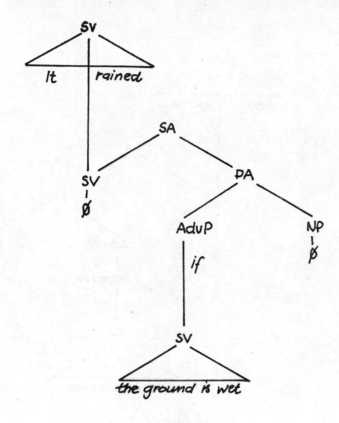

(c) (3)

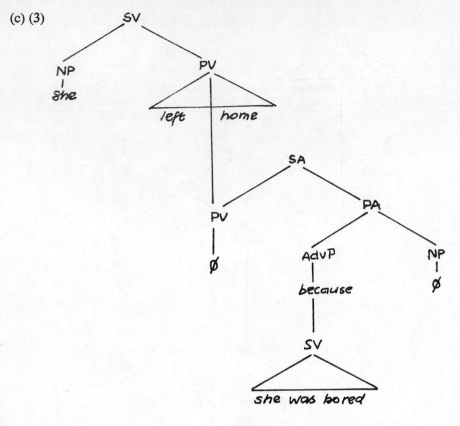

37. AdvP/PV

(a) Adverbial participles in -*ing* seem to be the output of this rule. They are identical to active participles (see rule 34) except that they modify predicative constituents.
(b) The child came up the walk pulling his wagon.

(c)

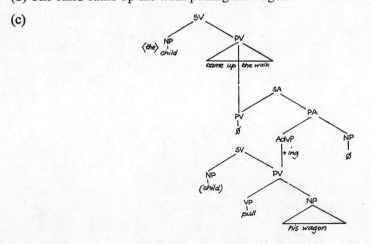

38. AdvP/VP PV

(a) Adverbs suffixed by *-ive* (*-ly*) can be attributed to this rule. They are like forms yielded by rule 35, but being adverbs they are often marked by *-ly*. Logical objects of the internal VP are marked by *of*.

(b) He read the report exclusive of the appendices.

(c)

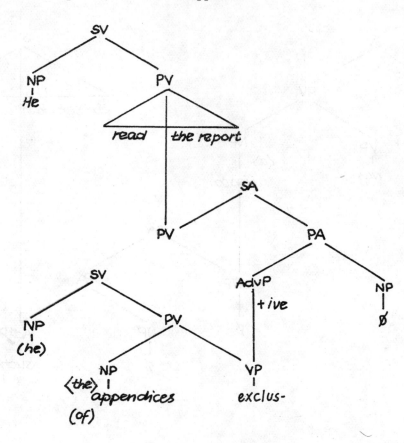

39. SV/AdjP PA

(a) This rule is the inversion of rule 33. It specifies a relative clause wherein a relative pro-adjective has the main clause as its antecedent.

(b) She sat down and cried, the party was such a fiasco (Inversion: The party was such a fiasco that she sat down and cried).

(c)

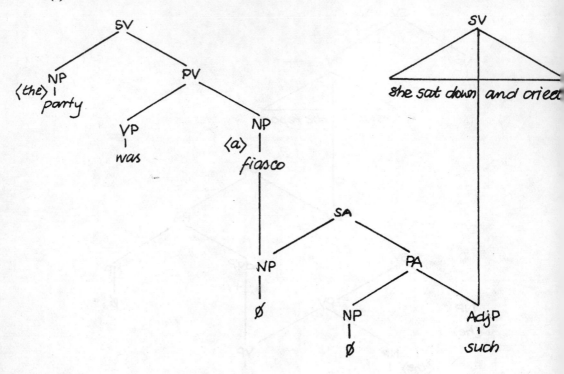

40. SV/AdvP PA

(a) This rule is the inversion of 36. It corresponds to structures where a relative pro-adverb has the main clause as its antecedent.

(b) It was cold, so I put on my gloves (Inversion: I put on my gloves because it was cold).

(c)

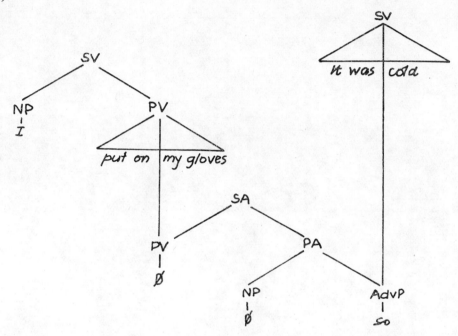

BIBLIOGRAPHY

Bach, Emmon
  1968   "Nouns and Noun Phrases", in: Bach and Harms (eds.), 1968.
Bach, Emmon and Robert T. Harms
  1968   *Universals in Linguistic Theory* (New York: Holt, Rinehart and Winston, Inc.).
Binnick, Robert I.
  1969   "An Application of an Extended Generative Semantic Model of Language to Man-machine
         Interaction" (Stockholm: Research Group for Quantitative Linguistics, Preprint No. 18)
         (A paper read at the International Conference on Computational Linguistics, 1969).
Bloomfield, Leonard
  1933   *Language* (New York: Holt, Rinehart and Winston, Inc.).
Carroll, John B.
  1964   *Language and Thought* (Englewood Cliffs, N.J.: Prentice-Hall, Inc.).
Chafe, Wallace L.
  1970   *Meaning and the Structure of Language* (Chicago: The University of Chicago Press).
Chomsky, Noam
  1957   *Syntactic Structures* (The Hague: Mouton and Co.).
  1965   *Aspects of the Theory of Syntax* (Cambridge, Mass.: MIT Press).
  1966   *Cartesian Linguistics, A Chapter in the History of Rationalist Thought* (New York: Harper
         and Row).
  1969   "Remarks on Nominalization" in: Jacobs and Rosenbaum (eds.), 1969.
Chomsky, Noam and Morris Halle
  1968   *The Sound Pattern of English* (New York: Harper and Row).
Emonds, Joseph
  1969   "Questions for Syntactic Research Raised by a Structure-Preserving Constraint on Trans-
         formations", presented at *Goals of Linguistic Theory*.
Gibb, Daryl
  1970   "Application of an Algorithm Based on the Set Theoretical Operations of Union and Inter-
         section to Machine Translation", unpublished master's thesis, Brigham Young University.
Goals of Linguistic Theory, Conference of the University of Texas at Austin, October 29–31,
  1969.
Hall, Barbara
  1963   Review of *Applikativnaja poroždajuščaja model' i isčislenie transformacij v russkom jazyke*,
         by S. K. Šaumjan and P. A. Sobol'ova (Moskva: Izdatel'stvo Akademii Nauk SSSR).
Jacobs, Roderick A. and Peter S. Rosenbaum
  1968   *English Transformational Grammar* (Waltham, Mass.: Blaisdell Publishing Co.).
  1969   *Readings in Transformational Grammar* (Waltham, Mass.: Ginn and Co.).
Katz, Jerrold J. and Paul M. Postal
  1964   An Integrated Theory of Linguistic Descriptions (Cambridge, Mass.: MIT Press).
Kuroda, S. Y.
  1968   "English Relativization and Certain Related Problems", *Language*, 44, 2 (Part I), June.

Lakoff, George
1965 *On the Nature of Syntactic Irregularity*, Report No. NSF-16 to the National Science Foundation (Cambridge, Mass.: The Computation Laboratory of Harvard University).
Langendoen, Terence D.
1969 *The Study of Syntax (The Generative-Transformational Approach to American English)* (New York: Holt, Rinehart and Winston, Inc.).
Lees, Robert B.
1966 *The Grammar of English Nominalizations* (The Hague: Mouton and Co.).
Lytle, Eldon G.
1971 "Structural Derivation in Russian", unpublished Ph.D. dissertation, University of Illinois (Champaign-Urbana).
Lytle, Eldon G. (ed.)
1971 *Interim Final Report: Research and Development in Linguistic Theory*, unpublished research report, Research Division Brigham Young University (Provo, Utah).
Lytle, Eldon G. and Melby, Alan K.
i. p. *Junction Grammar: Theory and Application* (The Hague: Mouton and Co.).
McCawley, J. D.
1968 "The Role of Semantics in Grammar", in: Bach and Harms (eds.), 1968.
Peters, Stanley
1969 "The Projection Problem: How is a Grammar to be Selected?", paper presented at *Goals in Linguistic Theory*.
Postal, Paul
1969 "The Best Theory", presented at *Goals in Linguistic Theory*.
Reichenbach, H.
1966 *Elements of Symbolic Logic* (New York: The McMillan Co.).
Rezvin, I. I.
1964 "Transformacionnyj analiz i transformacionnyj sintez", in: Šaumjan (ed.), 1964.
Robertson, John S.
1969 "Case Relationships in Mam Grammar", unpublished master's thesis, Brigham Young University.
Ross, J. R.
1967 "Constraints on Variables in Syntax", Ph.D. Dissertation (Cambridge, Mass.: MIT Press).
Šaumjan, S. K.
1964 "Transformacionnaja grammatika i applikativnaja poroždajuščaja model", in: Šaumjan (ed.), 1964.
Šaumjan, S. K. (ed.)
1964 *Transformacionnyj metod v strukturnoj lingvistike* (Moskva: Izdatel'stvo Nauka).
Waterman, John T.
1963 *Perspectives in Linguistics* (Chicago: The University of Chicago Press).

INDEX

A, 77
adjective, 48, 51, 75–77
adjectivalization, 66, 68–72
adjunction, 21 , 23, 27
adverb, 48, 63–64, 75–77
adverbialization, 66, 72–73
affix, 92
agreement, 92
all, 39–41
antecedent, 23, 24, 30–31, 75, 78, 82
as, 55–59, 103, 106
automatic translation, 89

base rule, 18, 36, 37
behaviorism, 85
by, 67, 68–70, 71

Cartesian product, 27
Chomsky, Noam, 15*fn*, 17, 19, 38*fn*, 55, 73, 87
clause, 31; see also *relative clause*
communication, 89
comparative, 13, 59–60
comparative linguistics, 89
competence, 7*fn*, 44*fn*
concept, 15
conceptual structure, 36
concord, 92
conjunction, 20, 21, 22–23, 30, 33, 35, 38, 41, 49–53, 77, 86
conjunction-reduction process, 23–27
context, 15

declarative, 34, 53
definitization, 29*fn*
deep structure, 19, 19*fn*, 37, 38, 42, 71
derivation, 31–32, 63–73
   lexical, 73

derived structure, 37
deverbal, 69–73
determination, 45*fn;* see also *restrictive clause*

embedding, 20, 23–29, 31, 55, 63, 71
evaluation measure (metric), 7–8
explication, 45*fn;* see also *nonrestrictive*

f eatures, 15, 42
   distinctive, 15, 42, 44, 47–48
   envelope, 33–35, 36, 49
   lexical, 15*fn*
   syntacto-semantic, 15*fn*, 20

generative semantics, 19
gerund, 63
grammar, 7, 7*fn*, 8, 86
grammatical rule, 23

hiatus, 23, 94, 101
Humboldt, Wilhelm von, 17, 17*fn*

imperative, 34
interrogative, 33–34, 49, 53
interrogative shift test (IST), 53, 56, 58–59
IST; see *interrogative shift test*

Jacobs, Roderick A., 32, 39
junction, 21–48
junction grammar, 90
junction rule (J-rule), 86
juncture, 40–41, 47

kernel, 35–36

137